THE STOCK B
OF THE
NENE VALLEY R/

A Guide to NVR Locomotives and
Rolling Stock
plus selected information on NVR Infrastructure.

Completely re-written 2007 Edition
By John Ginns
with contributions from David Harrison.

ISBN 1 - 903633 -06 -0

Published by the Nene Valley Railway Ltd.
Wansford Station, Stibbington, Peterborough, PE8 6LR
Tel: 01780 784444   Fax: 01780 784440
Registered Charity No. 263617.
Registered Museum No. 1636.

Typesetting, Design and Print Management by
Moorside Publishing Ltd.
2, Ringley Meadows, Bempton, Bridlington, YO15 1JR
Tel/Fax: 01262 851757

FOREWORD

Welcome to all readers to this the 2007 and latest edition of our Stock book. Previous editions have been well received and it is a number of years, some say too many, since the last edition went out of print. When you read this the railway will be celebrating or have celebrated its 30th anniversary in 2007.

The Nene Valley Railway is unique in that it is the only standard gauge heritage railway in the country that operates both British and Continental locomotives and carriages side by side. This book contains the information that will allow readers to identify and compare the rolling stock that makes up this unique collection. The photographs will allow easy identification and the text will inform both the enthusiast and layperson.

Without books like this there is a great danger that over time the true history of the rolling stock will be lost along with an understanding of why they are preserved. Hopefully this book will encourage you to take more interest and perhaps an active part in keeping such items in sound condition for future generations. It is sobering to think that when the first stock book was published in March 1981 rolling stock that held no interest to the enthusiasts of the day, with thousands of examples in daily use, can no longer be seen or even exist. The few that do still survive are treasured as museum exhibits.

The very first stock book for example contained only four small industrial diesel locomotives, whilst this edition has over ten listed. Many of you will not even remember seeing steam engines earning a living on the national rail network. The collection of locomotives and rolling stock not only changes over time but also continues to grow although a limiting factor is the amount of space that is available.

It is surprising how much time and effort goes into researching and bringing together the information to produce a publication like this and which will hopefully go a long way towards answering out visitor's questions. I would like to thank all those involved no matter how small their part in producing such a comprehensive record.

David D Jackson
Chairman
Nene Valley Railway
October 2006

CONTENTS
Page No.

CONTENTS - continued

INTRODUCTION
to the Nene Valley Railway Stock Book, 2007 Edition
by John W. Ginns

'Stock Book' is the traditional name for books like this, a term well enough understood by railway enthusiasts of all types. But we hope this book will also be of interest to the general visitor and the tourist with no particular interest in railways.

This book contains information on over 16 British and Continental main line and industrial steam locomotives, 14 main line and industrial diesel locomotives, 36 British and Continental passenger coaches, 70 freight vehicles, as well as Post Office, Engineering and Permanent Way rail vehicles, all to be found either working, on static display or receiving attention in the Nene Valley Railway Wansford Workshops.

The Nene Valley Railway is a *living* railway, part of the UK's living Heritage Railways movement, and with its unique stock of Continental locomotives and rolling stock, is also part of the *International* Heritage Railways scene. It is inevitable that within such a scenario, in any one year, there are bound to be movements of locomotives and rolling stock from one heritage line to another as well as 'new' stock coming in from the 'outside world' of UK Network Rail and beyond. Consequently, a book of this type can never remain 100% up-to-date even for one year.

In keeping with the spirit of heritage railways most dimensions and other technical data remain in imperial units, although this has meant, in some cases, data relating to Continental locomotives and rolling stock having been 'imperialised' from their original metric values. However, since ISO-metric units have long been part of the UK education system, a section on imperial - metric data conversion is now included,particularly for the use of visitors more familiar with the metric world. There is also a section dealing with the so-called *Berne Gauge* and other loading gauges used world-wide and there are drawings showing the gradient profile of the NVR line.

Some parts of the railway are, unfortunately, out-of-bounds to visitors, for Health and Safety reasons. If you can't find the locomotive, the wagon or whatever you are looking for on the railway - **please ask any member of staff.** They can usually be recognised by their NVR uniform, badge or hi-viz jacket/overalls - and occasionally, if they can find time for a short break, a cup of tea or coffee in one hand. We look forward to meeting you.

Any errors and omissions remain the responsibility of the current author and it would be appreciated if notification of any observed discrepancies, or new information or suggestions for inclusion in future editions be addressed to:

> Nene Valley Railway (Stock Book),
> Wansford Station,
> Stibbington,
> Peterborough,
> PE8 6LR.

ACKNOWLEDGMENTS

The Nene Valley Railway Stock book was first published in the spring of 1981 when NVR was in its fourth year of existence. Since then there have been numerous updates and new editions, the last being the wire-bound version compiled by David Harrison. Although this current edition is a complete re-write, it is built on the work of those earlier contributors and compilers who gathered together and presented an ever-growing wealth of information on the Railway's locomotives and rolling stock. So ACKNOWLEDGMENTS and a big *thank you* to all those concerned.

Fresh information for this 2007 Edition has, similarly, been provided by many people. These range from the owners or custodians of locomotives or items of rolling stock, to others with enthusiasm and dedication quietly beavering away in their corner of the Nene Valley Railway. Some have contributed small perhaps, but 'key' items of data, or ideas that have lead to larger 'finds'. Others have spent hours researching past records and setting down their work on paper for this book. Some have worked as individuals, whilst others represent groups of colleagues or organisations such as A1A Locomotives Ltd., the Iron and Steel Traction Group, our *Railworld* colleagues and, of course, the various working groups within the Nene Valley Railway itself. NVR's magazine *Nene Steam*, which often represents the only written record of locomotive and rolling stock refurbishment and overhaul work, has yielded much information for the updating of this book, so thanks are due to the authors of the Mechanical and Civil Engineering Group's Reports in that Magazine. Other contributors have obtained and passed on information anonymously.

Consequently it is virtually impossible to name and thank *everyone* who has contributed to this book in any way either with information or photographs, but the list includes the following, arranged alphabetically - Alex Alder, Martin Bell, Neil Boden, Richard Busby, Jon Cooper, Richard Fearne, Brian Hallett, David Harrison, David Hartley, Steve Harvey, David Head, Barbara Hoffmann, Gordon Kobish, Roger Manns, Robert Maskill, Gordon Maslin, Belinda Moncaster, Andrew Neale, Rev. Richard Paten, Brian Pearce, Gary Walker, Peter Waszak, Alan Whenman, Brian White, John Whitehead, David Withers, ... and *thank you* to all those other contributors whose names have slipped through the net.

We should not fail to collectively acknowledge the enormous source of information available through the many past and present railway publications - the books, journals and periodicals, far too many to list, written by and for railway people of all stations in life - and the contribution their writers make to the pool of information on railway matters. This book is well provided with data from such sources. In the same vein, rapidly coming to the forefront as a source of information on just about everything, certainly including railways, is the Internet, which has provided data for this book on such diverse subjects as Toby the Tram Engine and the Berne Gauge. Thanks also to Hannah Hackett, Brian White, Beccy Caffrey, Jonathan Headland, Cris Rees and the other staff in the NVR Office, for providing support and down-to-earth guidance in compiling this Edition and for checking through the new layout and proof reading. Last but by no means least, thanks to Margaret and Edwin Craggs of Moorside Publishing, who undertook the typesetting, design, scanning, print management and turning a bundle of ever-changing pages into this book.

John Ginns.

Abbreviations and Notations used in this Book

BR   British Rail or British Railways.
BSC   British Steel Corporation or British Sugar Corporation - as appropriate.
DB   Deutsches Bundesbahn (German Federal Railways).
DR   Deutsches Reichesbahn (East German Railways).
DSB   Danske Statsbaner (Danish State Railways).
GER   Great Eastern Railway.
GNR   Great Northern Railway.
GWR   Great Western Railway.
LMS   London, Midland and Scottish Railway.
LNER   London and North Eastern Railway.
LNWR   London and North Western Railway.
MR   Midland Railway.
NSB   Norges Statsbaner (Norwegian State Railways).
PKP   Polskie Koleje Paostwowe (Polish State Railways).
SJ   Statens Jämvägar (Swedish State Railways).
SNCB   Societe Nationale des Chemins de Fer Belges (Belgian National Railways).
SNCF   Societe Nationale des Chemins de Fer Francais (French National Railways)
SR   Southern Railway.
TOPS   Total Operating Processing System (BR computerised stock control system)
hp/bhp Horse power/brake horse power.   ′   Feet.
lb or lbf Pounds or pounds force.   ″   Inches.
mph   Miles per hour.   **mm** Millimetres.
psi   Pounds per square inch.   **m**   Metres
rev/min. Revolutions per minute.

Other abbreviations used are explained at the relevant places in the text.
Steam and Diesel Engine Cylinder Dimensions.
Dimensions quoted are diameter of cylinder and length of piston stroke.
Thus 14″ x 24″ indicates 14″ cylinder diameter x 24″ Stroke.

Locomotive Wheel Arrangements:
The Whyte notation is used to indicate wheel arrangements for steam locomotives and diesel locomotives not having bogie wheels.
Numbers separated by hyphens indicate the number of wheels possessed by a loco-motive. Thus **4-6-2** denotes 4 carrying wheels at the front, 6 coupled driving wheels and 2 carrying wheels at the rear (front oo-OOO-o rear).
0-4-0 denotes a locomotive with 4 coupled driving wheels only (OO).
T indicates side water tanks; **ST** indicates a 'saddle' tank; **VB** - vertical boiler.
Diesel locomotives having bogie wheels use a number to indicate the number of non-powered (carrier) axles and a capital letter followed by a small 'o' to indicate the number of independently-powered axles per bogie, the exception being 'A' on its own indicating an independently powered axle.
Thus **1Co-Co1** indicates one bogie set having one non-powered leading axle followed by 3 axles each with their own traction motor. The other bogie set is iden-tical, but mounted the other way round.
A1A-A1A indicates a locomotive having two 3-axle bogies, with front and rear axles on each bogie having traction motors, and the centre axle of each bogie being a non-powered carrier.

Nene Valley Railway Locomotives - Introduction

Main Line Steam* Locomotives.
Although the Nene Valley Railway's collection of locomotives is not the largest in the United Kingdom, it is without doubt the most diverse, with a strong international flavour, for the NVR is an *international* railway. Ranging from the once commonplace LNER 'B1' *Mayflower* and Class 5MT *City of Peterborough*, both 4-6-0s, to the massive 2-10-0 Austrian-built *Kreigslok* and the Danish 0-6-0 *Tinkerbell*, itself based on an original British design of 1873, there is something to interest the most demanding of main line steam locomotive enthusiasts and historians.

Industrial Steam* Locomotives.
Industrial steam locomotives are well represented. There are two ex-ironstone quarry locomotives, once belonging to that rural industry centred around the world of machinery we now refer to as *classic quarry plant*, the world of Ruston Bucyrus and Ransomes and Rapier rope-operated face shovels and draglines, slowly following steam locomotives into history. Other NVR 'industrials' include locomotives with mixed careers in the wartime Ministry of Defence, civil engineering construction, open cast coal working and the sugar beet industry. The latter dates back to those days when the farmer would cart his sugar beet harvest to the local station sidings, to be loaded into rail wagons, collected by the local pick-up goods train and hauled to the nearest sugar beet factory, finally to be shunted in the processing plant by locomotives now represented on the Nene Valley Railway by Avonside *No. 1945* and Hudswell Clarke *Derek Crouch* and the original *Thomas*.

* See also Appendix B, page 116, for a brief explanation of locomotive steam boiler certification referred to in this book under the various steam locomotive descriptions.

Main Line and Industrial Diesel Locomotives.
Diesel locomotives have long since earned their place in the world of heritage railways and the Nene Valley Railway has a representative collection of diesel-mechanical, diesel-hydraulic and diesel-electric main line and industrial locomotives. At least 6 of our diesels have seen service in the ironstone quarrying industry. Like steam locomotives, each type or class is individual - in fact there must be more variations in diesel locomotive designs than there ever were in steam locomotives - and the features of each are described in each entry. NVR's smallest diesel locomotive, in terms of nominal engine power, is No. 2896 "Frank" @ 35 bhp. The largest is the Type 5 Class 56 diesel-electric 3,250 bhp, easily the most powerful locomotive on the Nene Valley Railway.

Working and Stored Locomotives.
Unfortunately, as on all heritage railways, not all of our locomotives are in working order at any one time. A selection of steam and diesel locomotives is in regular use on NVR trains and the remainder can usually be seen either in Wansford Yard sidings or receiving attention in our workshops.

Ownership of Locomotives.
Heritage railways do not normally 'own' all the locomotives that run on their lines. Some are owned by private individuals or by owning - groups, their locomotives being regarded as 'resident' on a particular railway, although from time to time some locomotives are moved from one 'home' to another. Such particulars are given in each locomotive entry.

New Locomotive Overhaul Workshop.
In early 2006 the Mechanical Engineering Department announced the imminent construction at Wansford of a new 134' x 60' locomotive heavy overhaul workshop, with a 10 ton overhead crane. The initial details that accompanied this announcement were published in *Nene Steam No. 81*, and subsequent issues can be expected to carry progress reports on this project.

In addition to providing much improved working conditions and facilities, it is hoped that this development will free part of the 'old' workshop to provide undercover protection for locomotives and other rail vehicles that currently have to be left in the open awaiting eventual attention.

Updated information on the work of the Mechanical Engineering Department, including progress reports on locomotives, carriages and other NVR rolling stock, can be found in NVR's magazine *Nene Steam*, and at the regularly updated website **www.nvr.org.uk/groups/mechanical**

See page 7 for abbreviations and notations used in this book.

A busy scene on the new workshop building site on 10th June 2006.
Photo: E. Craggs.

British Main Line Steam
Locomotive No. 73050   'City of Peterborough'   Class 5MT 4-6-0

Country of Origin: United Kingdom
Builders: British Railways, Derby. Year: 1954
Number of cylinders: 2 (19″ x 28″). Boiler pressure: 225 psi
Driving wheels diameter: 6′ 2″.
Weight 126 tons. Train brakes: Air/vacuum
Original owner: British Railways (SR). Current owner: Peterborough City Council.

Origins.

No. 73050 was one of 172 such locomotives designed by R A Riddles as a develop-ment of the Stanier 'Black Fives'. 73050 had cost £19,655 to build, complete with ten-der and entered service on 14th April 1954.

The locomotive was chosen for display, in its BR lined black livery, at the 1954 International Railway Congress Willesden Exhibition. After the Exhibition 73050 was allocated to Bath Green Park for working to Bournemouth on the heavy gradients of the Somerset and Dorset Line. It was reallocated to Shrewsbury in 1964 before being placed in store. In 1966, 73050 was moved to Manchester Agecroft and then on to Patricroft, finally being withdrawn from service in July 1968, having run for well over half a million miles and having been 'spotter reported' as being seen on every region of British Railways.

Preservation.

In search of a suitable locomotive to put on permanent static display in Peterborough as a memorial to the age of steam, the Rev. Richard Paten, of Peterborough, visited Patricroft Locomotive Depot, Manchester, accompanied by Harry Botterill, a Peterborough New England Depot Foreman. Acting on the advice of Harry, who knew the locomotive to be in good condition, Richard Paten purchased 73050 for £3,000. John McIntyre, Principal of Peterborough Regional College offered a site at the College, in which Richard Paten expressed interest.

73050 travelled under its own steam from Manchester, arriving at Peterborough before midnight on 11th September 1968, having been delivered at night to avoid adverse publicity.

However, it was soon realised that the locomotive was in too good a condi-tion to be 'wasted' standing on a plinth. It remained for 3 weeks at New England Shed and was then transferred to a siding at Peterborough East Station under the care of the East Anglian Locomotive Preservation Society (later the Peterborough Locomotive Society), where BR generously provided 6 months accommodation free of charge. In the spring of 1969 Baker Perkins offered a site on their private siding adjacent to the East Coast Main Line, where 73050 then stood until 1971 and must have been seen by literally millions of rail passengers travelling north, south, east and west through Peterborough.

On closure of Baker Perkins' siding in 1971, 73050 moved on again - this time to siding space offered by the British Sugar Corporation at their Woodston site, off Oundle Road. It was here that 73050 came into the care of the Peterborough Railway Society who had their working base at the same site. In 1972 the Peterborough Locomorive Society became the Peterborough Railway Society and then the locomotive was steamed for the first time in preservation. Soon afterwards, on 28th August 1972, it was officially named *City of Peterborough* by the Mayor of Peterborough, Councillor Roy Topley.

To the Nene Valley Railway

In 1973, 73050's owner, Richard Paten, donated the locomotive to Peterborough City Council on the understanding that it would be leased to the Nene Valley Railway for 99 years. Thus, in a sense, now with the custody of a main line locomotive, began the NVR story.

Until 1975, 73050 operated trains at Wansford Station on NVR Open Days. In 1977 a thorough refurbishment was required, with Peter Brotherhood of Peterborough carrying out the task at their Walton Works. With the work completed, in July 1980, 73050 returned to Orton Mere from New England, via the Fletton Loop, in immaculate Brunswick Green and hauled by a BR Class 08 diesel locomotive.

On 30th June 1986, to mark the opening of the NVR Peterborough Extension, 73050 entered the new Peterborough Nene Valley Station from the west driven by Prince Edward.

The locomotive was withdrawn from service in 1988 on expiry of its boiler certificate. Thus began first the wait, the dismantling and inspection and then the long, slow task of rebuilding and return to steam. 73050 was worked on throughout the 1990s whenever the small staff of paid fitters and the handful of volunteers could find the time, in between essential maintenance and repair work on NVR's in-service locomotives. The work required on 73050 turned out to be extensive. Many new parts had to be made, some 'in-house' at Wansford workshops, others by outside specialists. Some bought-in parts, made to original BR Standard Class 5 drawings, would not fit as the original mating parts on the locomotive were found to be non-standard - so much for 1950s Quality Assurance! Included in the wide-ranging work required were complete new cab panels, manufactured and riveted together at Wansford and attention to the air and vacuum braking systems which were extensively re-worked.

To save 'boiler certificate time' the decision was made to temporarily refit the boiler to the frame so that newly-made pipe runs and other fittings could be trial-assembled. At the same time the new smoke box was trial-fitted allowing line-up holes to be drilled. The boiler lagging was also given its 'first fitting' at this stage, enabling some of the new panels to be re-made to fit properly. Then, of course, all had to be dismantled and the boiler removed from the frame again, for insurance inspection and test access.

At long last, in late 2004, 73050's boiler passed its hydraulic and steam tests. In January 2005 work began first to finally refit the boiler to the locomotive frame, followed by the associated pipework, fittings and lagging. The earlier 'trial' fitting of the boiler, piping and fittings turned out to be a wise decision indeed, in time saved when final assembly was carried out.

As assembly continued unavoidable 'challenges' were dealt with as they arose. Additional work was found, for example, to be required on the firebox doors, taking several days to sort out rather than the couple of hours anticipated.

Finally, the cab, controls and other 'body work', fittings and 'cosmetics' were reunited on the locomotive frame. At the same time the tender, which had also been virtually rebuilt from scratch, was completed and ready for coupling to the locomotive.

Meanwhile, in late 1999 the NVR membership had been invited to cast their votes as to whether the locomotive should be repainted in BR lined Brunswick Green, the livery in which it had worked on NVR until its withdrawal from service, or in BR lined black, its livery when new in 1954. 414 votes were cast, 217 in favour of BR black and 197 in support of Brunswick Green.

73050s steam was raised 'for real' on 26th May 2005, the first time in almost 18 years and 'disguised' as a continental locomotive, was used the following month for the TV filming of Agatha Christie's Poirot *The Mystery of the Blue Train*.

73050 *City of Peterborough*, at age 51, was officially back into NVR service on 2nd July 2005 - in its original British Railways lined black livery.

No. 73050, City of Peterborough on TPO duty 10th June 2006.   Photo: E. Craggs

No. 1306 "Mayflower" LNER Class B1 on TPO duties at Wansford 17th June 2006.
Photo: David Harrison

Locomotive No. 1306　　'Mayflower'　　Class B1 4-6-0

Country of origin: United Kingdom
Builders: North British Locomotive Company, Glasgow. Year 1948.
Number of cylinders: 2 (20″ x 26″). Boiler pressure: 225 psi.
Driving wheels diameter: 6′ 2″. Weight: 123 tons 13 cwt.
Train Brakes: Vacuum
Original owner: LNER/British Railways. Current owner: Gerald Boden.

The Class B1 mixed traffic locomotives were first introduced in 1942 by LNER Engineer Edward Thompson, to replace the many ageing engines of similar type, as Sir Nigel Gresley had only B17s under the 4-6-0 heading, but these were not mixed traffic locomotives.

B1s frequently appeared on the original Nene Valley Northampton - Peterborough services in British Railways days.

No. 1306 was built by the North British Locomotive Co., Glasgow, as part of a batch of 150 locomotives ordered in January 1946. No. 1306 entered service with *British Railways* painted on the tender and the number 61306 on the cab side.

61306 was first allocated to Hull Botanic Gardens. In June 1959 it was transferred to Hull Dairycoates and finally, in June 1967, to Low Moor, just south of Bradford. On 30th September 1967 it was withdrawn from service and eventually sold to private buyers in preservation, being based at Steamtown, Carnforth.

During its service with British Railways No. 61306 was eventually painted black, but after arriving at Carnforth was repainted in LNER Apple Green livery once again, which it continues to carry at the present time.

The name *Mayflower* was originally carried by another B1 locomotive, No. 61379, which worked from Immingham and along the ECML through Peterborough. Although this locomotive was eventually scrapped, the name *Mayflower* was applied to 1306 during preservation, to continue the association of the two towns of Boston, Lincolnshire and Massachusetts, USA, commemorating the voyage of the Pilgrim Fathers, over 400 years ago.

During the time at Carnforth Locomotive 1306 was used on main line specials and took part in the Shildon Cavalcade in 1975. In 1978 the locomotive was purchased by Gerald Boden and moved to the Great Central Railway where it stayed until 1989, when it moved to its original shed at Hull Dairycoates under the HLPG banner. When the site was sold for development No. 1306 was moved to Wansford on 16th May 1991, to complete its overhaul.

The locomotive entered service on the Nene Valley Railway in 2003.

Country of origin: United Kingdom
Builders: Hunslet Engine Company, Leeds (No. 2855). Year 1943
Number of cylinders: 2 (18" x 26"). Boiler pressure: 170 psi.
Driving wheels diameter: 4' 3". Weight: 48 tons. Brakes: Air/vacuum
Original owner: Ministry of Defence. Current owner: Nene Valley Railway.

Developed from the Class 50550 prototypes, the Hunslet Austerity tank locomotives were designed to meet the requirements of the wartime Ministry of Defence for a powerful yet simple and robust locomotive (*austere* = enforced simplicity) for shunting and short trip working both within the UK and overseas. As such, these locomotives were given a life expectancy of only two years. This particular machine was originally numbered WD No. 75006 and is the earliest example of this class to be preserved.

After its wartime service 75006 was allocated to the Ministry of Fuel and Power. In 1952 it was sold to Derek Crouch (Contractors) Ltd., who used it in various open-cast coal sites in Northumberland. In 1968 the locomotive was moved to Onllwyn, Glamorgan, also for open-cast coal site work, where it remained in regular use until 1973. It was then taken out of service, standing spare and in 1976 was presented to the Nene Valley Railway by Derek Crouch Ltd., on indefinite loan.

In 1979 rebuilding of the locomotive commenced and was completed in 1984. NVR decided that as 75006 was similar to the 75 purchased by the LNER in 1946, it should be re-numbered to BR68081 after the 68006 to 68080 series.

In 1995, after its ten year overhaul, the locomotive lost its BR identity, being repainted red and renumbered 75006. It remained in regular use hauling NVR passenger trains until 2005, when its ten year boiler certificate expired once again. It has now taken its place in the 'rebuild queue' at Wansford.

No. 75006 at Wansford on 10th June 2006.   Photo: E. Craggs

British Industrial Steam Locomotive No. 1800	'Thomas'	0-6-0T

Country of origin: United Kingdom
Builders: Hudswell Clarke Ltd., Leeds. Year: 1947
Number of cylinders: 2 (16" x 24"). Boiler pressure: 160 psi.
Driving wheels diameter: 3' 9". Weight: 41 tons 17cwt.
Train brakes: Air/vacuum.
Original owner: British Sugar Corporation, Peterborough.
Current owner: Nene Valley Railway.

A unique Thomas Story - Origins.

This originally un-named Hudswell Clarke 0-6-0 tank locomotive was built in 1947, but from the outset was allocated the number 1800 which it retains to this day.

The story of the design for this locomotive goes back to the First World War period, when, in 1914 Hudswell Clarke Ltd. designed a simple, but rugged 0-6-0 tank locomotive specifically for the Port of London Authority (PLA), which then operated a considerable mileage of railways serving the Royal, Millwall and Tilbury Dock Groups. The initial order was for five locomotives, Hudswell Clarke giving them Works Nos. 1101 to 1105 and all five had been dispatched to PLA by 15th March 1915. The locomotives were clearly a success as repeat orders followed from PLA, with a final total of 24, the last two being delivered to PLA as late as 1954 - nearly 40 years after the first ones!

This Hudswell Clarke 'PLA' locomotive type was adopted as a standard industry design and amongst other applications 14 were built for the National Coal Board between 1948 and 1955. An order for one such locomotive was received from the British Sugar Corporation and as a consequence Locomotive No. 1800 was delivered to the BSC sugar factory, Woodston, Peterborough, on 30th June 1947. Here it was to remain all its industrial working life and had the honour of being the largest in BSC's locomotive fleet.

No. 1800 was in daily use during the sugar beet season pushing wagons loaded with sugar-beet fresh from the area's farms, up the steep gradients to the unloading flumes, as well as marshalling lengthy trains in BSC's extensive sidings. These sidings, incidentally, were situated off the Fletton Loop which branches away from the present Nene Valley Railway just east of Orton Mere Station.

In the late 1960s No. 1800 was replaced by a diesel locomotive for every-day duties, but was maintained in good working order by the regular driver Harry Tassell. However, No. 1800 was regularly put back to work during the peak of BSC's annual autumn-spring sugar beet processing campaign and continued in this role until 1973, when the locomotive suffered damage to its firebox and had to be permanently taken out of use.

Thomas is named.

Three years earlier, however, in 1970, the newly formed Peterborough Railway Society (in effect the predecessor of the Nene Valley Railway) had set up their working base in a compound within BSC's sidings and the members' attention was immediately drawn to Locomotive No. 1800. Because of its even-then immaculate blue livery, they nicknamed it _Thomas_, Rev. W. Awdry's famous children's creation, by then 23 years old and coincidentally, the same age as No. 1800, both having been built/first published, respectively, in 1947.

The 'friendly' blue locomotive was a familiar sight to BSC Open Day visitors and in 1971 the name *Thomas* was officially bestowed upon BSC locomotive No. 1800 by the Rev. Awdry himself, at the BSC National Sport and Family Day that year. The locomotive, now officially *Thomas*, continued to give visitors short brake van rides at BSC Open Days, between its annual, intermittent BSC 'industrial' duties until, in 1973, it had to be taken out of service with firebox damage, referred to earlier.

To the Nene Valley Railway.

In a generous gesture, BSC sold the locomotive to Peterborough Railway Society (who, it may seem in hindsight, had notionally 'adopted' *Thomas* anyway!) for a nominal £100.

The Society stored *Thomas* for several years until eventually parts, including a good boiler, from a similar locomotive (No. 1844 and presumably one of the 14 Hudswells originally sold to NCB, referred to above), were purchased from NCB Whitwood Colliery, Yorkshire and the task of rebuilding by the Society engineers could begin.

By 1979 *Thomas* was back in action again, as a major attraction at the newly-formed Nene Valley Railway at Wansford.

In the 1980s *Thomas* visited the Great Western Society at Didcot. So great were crowds that turned out to see the now famous engine that the police had to be called to control the traffic. *Thomas* also made visits to Leicester and Cambridge to promote the Nene Valley Railway and at a BR Open day at Cambridge in September 1990, even took part in running a shuttle service under the overhead electric wires. For its size, no other railway locomotive can have attracted so much public attention.

In 1986 the BSC's Peterborough diesel shunter had failed and Thomas returned to his old home, just for one day whilst the diesel was repaired, to carry out his old duties as a shunter once again. So just as the Rev. Awdry's stories tell, *Thomas* was first ousted from his duties by a 'modern' diesel locomotive but then had to go back to work at his old job when the diesel broke down!

It has been suggested that this was probably the very last occasion in British industrial history when a steam locomotive worked in factory sidings.

In the early 1990s, with its ten-year boiler certificate expired, *Thomas* underwent a major overhaul by NVR's Wansford engineers, but work on major items was contracted out. The wheels, for example, were reworked by a Chatham based specialist firm, whilst the boiler work was carried out at Swindon at a cost of many thousands of pounds. During this rebuild vacuum brake equipment was fitted to the locomotive.

Back at work again and another new generation of children. Thomas' popularity at Wansford never ceased and there were many demands for him to make public appearances. He performed 'civic duties' in Peterborough, when called upon to participate in switching on the Christmas lights; an apt choice as *Thomas* is a truly local personality. At his Wansford home as many as 8,000 visitors turned out to see him on just one working weekend. On one occasion during this period Thomas left the Nene Valley Railway to visit *Thomas* events at Broxbourne, Hertfordshire. Although he was not able to be in steam, hundreds of people queued for up to an hour just to pay a visit to his footplate.

Every year *Thomas* celebrates his birthday in June, holding a big party at Wansford for all his young friends and their families and in 2001 he reached the grand old age of 30 as *Thomas* (and 54 as a locomotive).

Another rebuild.

February 2002, another ten years on and time for another boiler inspection, test, another ten year certificate and another rebuild. This time, in the light of NVR Wansford workshop staff's other commitments *Thomas* was sent away to 'hospital' and at a cost of nearly £100,000 (most of it for specialist boiler work, but fortunately partly met by a Heritage Lottery Grant) returned ready for work in Spring 2004, to be welcomed back by yet another generation of children and their parents.

Thomas sees regular use at special events such as *Thomas* Weekends, at school half terms and at Easter, as well as carrying out shunting duties in Wansford Yard. When he's not working he is usually standing in platform 1, Wansford station. Not having been designed for continuous 'main line' passenger train working he doesn't very often make the run to Peterborough, although during 2004 he did run several 'Big Adventure' trains to Peterborough, working to a slowed-down timetable. His normal *Thomas* trains make the shorter journey from Wansford station through the 'haunted' Wansford Tunnel to Yarwell Junction and back again. With the anticipated opening of the new Yarwell Station in late 2006, *Thomas'* passengers will be able to leave the train at Yarwell, to visit the 'countryside at the end of the line' and wait for Thomas and his next train back to Wansford.

Locomotive 'purists' may scorn the 'faces' attached to *Thomas'* smoke box door and to the noses and smoke box doors of his locomotive friends, but perhaps we all need to be reminded that railways can mean quite different things to people of different ages and different backgrounds and of course to each new generation.

So harking back to that day in 1971 at the British Sugar Corporation Sidings, Peterborough, when the Rev. Awdry gave Locomotive No. 1800 its name, the Nene Valley Railway can be justly proud to own and operate the original real, live, steaming **Thomas** and will continue to welcome to Wansford each new generation of children and their families, to see and to ride behind this most famous of all small railway engines.

Thomas **and Autism**

The significance of *Thomas the Tank Engine*, as presented in the Rev. Awdry's original children's books and by TV, videos, DVDs and *Thomas* toys, *for children with Autism and Asperger syndrome*, is well researched, and published by The National Autistic Society and other bodies.

No suggestion whatsoever of any significance to such children of the real, life-size, steaming, noisy *Thomas* is implied by the Nene Valley Railway - such matters await responsible, scientific research. However, parents/guardians of children with Autism and Asperger sydrome and who are not already aware of this association with the literary *Thomas,* may wish to contact The National Autistic Society at 393 City Road, London, EC1V 1NG or visit their web site: **www.nas.org.uk** for more information.

No. 1800, 'Thomas' basks in the sun in Wansford Yard 19 June 2006.

Photo: E. Craggs

No. 1953, 'Jacks Green' on display at Wansford.   Photo: R. Maskill

Locomotive No. 1953   'Jacks Green'   0-6-0ST

Country of origin: United Kingdom.
Builders: Hunslet Engine Company, Leeds. Year: 1939.
No. of cylinders: 2 (16″ x 22″).   Boiler Pressure: 160 psi.
Driving wheels diameter: 3′9″. Weight: 39 tons.
Train brakes: Air / vacuum.
Original owner: Nassington Barrowden Mining Company, Nassington, Northants.
Current owner: Nene Valley Railway.

Jacks Green was purchased for and spent all its industrial life at Nassington Ironstone Quarries, just three miles west of Wansford, on the former Market Harborough line. It was in this rural industrial scenario that *Jacks Green* spent over 30 years hauling loaded standard-gauge iron ore tipplers, three or four at a time, out of the quarries to make up longer trains for main line dispatch and as required, hauling the quarry company's own loaded hopper wagons from the quarry faces, for discharging onto the calcine clamps, prior to main line dispatch.

Jacks Green and its sister engine *Ring Haw* (now on the North Norfolk Railway) were the last remaining steam locomotives in ironstone service in England when the quarries closed in 1970.

Jacks Green was delivered in steam to the Peterborough Railway Society base at Peterborough Sugar Factory on 1st January 1971.

Following several years' service at PRS Open Days at the Sugar Factory and later at NVR Wansford, the locomotive was completely overhauled during 1976-77 by the apprentices at Peter Brotherhood Ltd. and repainted in LNER Apple Green livery by a group of Society members. This work completed, *Jacks Green* returned to Wansford via the BR main line and Fletton Loop. The locomotive was fitted with air braking equipment during 1980.

In 1987 *Jacks Green* was taken out of traffic until funds will allow a complete overhaul, but the locomotive still masquerades, out of steam, as *Percy* during *Thomas* Weekends.

During 1993 *Jacks Green* was repainted to a darker shade of green. Still 'in the queue' for eventual restoration, the locomotive has in the meantime, been given a cab 'face lift', for use as a static educational display. A protective screen is to be fitted to provide mutual protection of the controls and over-enthusiastic little hands, but this screen will be removed for supervised 'instructional' visits. In this role *Jacks Green* will be on display in a specially constructed platform extension adjacent to Wansford station building.

British Industrial Steam
Locomotive No. 39   'Rhos'   0-6-0ST

Country of origin: United Kingdom.
Builders: Hudswell Clarke & Company Limited, Leeds. (1308). Year: 1918.
Number of cylinders: 2 (15″ x 22″). Boiler Pressure: 160 psi.
Driving wheels diameter: 3′7″. Weight: 25 tons.
Original owner: Lloyds Ironstone Company, Corby.
Current owner: Gerald Boden.

No. 39 was ordered by Lloyds Ironstone Co. on 22nd November 1917 and was delivered new on 15th January 1918. The locomotive was eventually absorbed into the Stewarts and Lloyds Company and then, with nationalisation of the steel industry, into the British Steel Corporation. The locomotive operated in the Glendon and Corby areas hauling heavy ore trains considerable distances, hence the full mechanical lubrication system.

After diesel locomotives took over the work (including four Class 14s that were eventually to come to the Nene Valley Railway) *Rhos* was sold and displayed for many years at Burnham Market. It was eventually bought by its present owner and stored at the Rutland Railway Museum, Cottesmore, then moved to NVR Wansford to join *Mayflower,* also belonging to the same owner.

Rhos requires a full overhaul which is expected to commence now that *Mayflower* is back in steam.

A Sad looking No. 39, 'Rhos' awaits restoration in Wansford Shed.   Photo: B. Hallett

Locomotive No. 1539 'Derek Crouch' 0-6-0ST

Country of origin: United Kingdom.
Builder: Hudswell Clarke & Company Ltd., Leeds. Year: 1924.
Number of cylinders: 2 (10" x 20"). Boiler pressure: 160 psi.
Driving wheels diameter: 3'9". Weight: 24 tons.
Original owner: Sir Robert McAlpine & Sons at BSC Wissington, Norfolk.
Current owner: Nene Valley Railway.

Locomotive No. 1539, built in 1924, was used from new by Sir Robert McAlpine &
Sons on the construction of Wissington Sugar Beet Factory near Downham Market,
Norfolk, the factory itself being opened in 1925. The locomotive was presumably
then sold to the British Sugar Corporation* as it was subsequently used on the
Wissington Light Railway. This was a remarkable network of lines that connected
the factory with the LNER Stoke Ferry Branch, as well as with the many farms in the
neighbouring Fen region by means of tracks laid along the edges of the fields. At this
time No. 1539 was named *Hayle* but was subsequently renamed *Wissington Loco*.

In 1955 the locomotive was sold to Derek Crouch (Contractors) Ltd, (who
had their bases at Newcastle, Peterborough and Melbourne, Australia) for use at
their open cast coal working at Widdrington, Northumberland.

Now named *Derek Crouch* the locomotive remained in Northumberland
until 1970, when it was placed in store at Eye near Peterborough. In 1972 the locomotive was transferred on permanent loan to Peterborough Railway Society, who
restored it to Derek Crouch house colours (maroon and cream) and returned it to
steam in August 1973.

In April 1974 *Derek Crouch* worked the first train along the Nene Valley
Railway under the auspices of Peterborough Railway Society and subsequently
appeared regularly at Society Steam Days.

On expiry of its boiler certificate and also in need of further attention, No.
1539 was placed on display at the main NVR Wansford Centre entrance, but has now
been transferred to a siding in Wansford Yard, pending a decision as to its future.

* It seems that the predecessors of the British Sugar Corporation had a close association with Locomotive builders Hudswell Clarke through two routes. Not only did
they purchase Hudswell Clarke locomotives directly, as with No. 1800 *Thomas*, but
civil engineering contractors Sir Robert McAlpine & Sons were frequent users of
Hudswell Clarke locomotives and used them during the construction of sugar beet
factories in the region. On completion of the work several of these locomotives were
sold on to the sugar beet factories for use in their sidings. So the early history of locomotive No. 1539, later *Derek Crouch,* is by no means unique.

BSC's Wissington Sugar Beet Factory, No. 1539s first place of work, is still
active and is BSC's largest plant. All sugar beet is now taken in by road - the factory can accommodate up to 900 lorry loads per day.

No. 1539 'Derek Crouch' awaits his future in a Wansford siding.

Photo: Robert Maskill

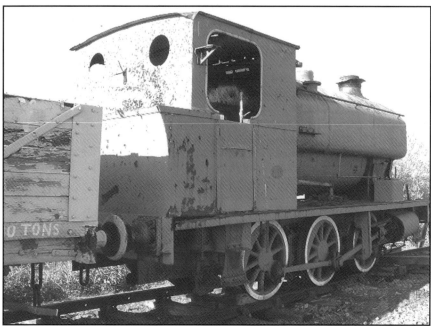

No. 1945 before being moved to Wansford for restoration.   Photo: Brian Hallett

British Industrial Steam	
Locomotive No. 1945	**Class B4 0-6-0ST**

Country of origin: United Kingdom.
Builders: Avonside Engine Company, Bristol. Year: 1926.
Number of cylinders: 2 (14″ x 24″). Boiler pressure: 160 psi.
Driving wheels diameter: 3′ 8″. Weight 28 tons.
Original owner: Central Sugar Company Ltd., Peterborough.
Current owner: Tony Goulding.

Released from the Avonside Locomotive Works on 25th October 1926, No. 1945 was purchased for the opening of the Peterborough Sugar factory that same year. It worked there until 1947 when it was transferred to Kings Lynn Sugar Factory upon the arrival at Peterborough of Locomotive No. 1800 (later to become *Thomas*).

No. 1945 was used regularly at Kings Lynn until 1970 and in 1971 was presented by the British Sugar Corporation to Peterborough Railway Society.

During the building of the NVR Peterborough Extension No. 1945 was placed at the eastern end of the line painted in a bright green, bearing the legend 'Into - City'. When the extension came into regular use the locomotive remained there, at the buffer stops, painted in eye-catching red, with *'Nene Valley Railway'* painted on the tank sides, attracting the attention of passengers on the East Coast Main and the March lines.

The locomotive was subsequently moved back to Wansford, where, due to the shortage of covered space it stood for many years on static display in the siding to the east of Wansford signal box, in view of passengers in passing NVR trains.

However, in January 2006 No. 1945 was moved into Wansford Yard where it can now be seen and where, in spite of its alleged 'scrap' condition, work has commenced on dismantling the locomotive with a view to eventually restoring it to full steaming condition. Many parts are missing and replacements will have to be sourced or made from new. However the small team undertaking this work have experience in having restored a similar locomotive elsewhere.

Offers of practical help with this restoration and/or information on the availability of 'spares' will be welcome.

Further information on this project can be found at **www.ab2157.org.uk.** through which the owner can also be contacted.

| Continental Main Line Steam |
| Locomotive No. 52-7173 'Kriegslok'   Class 52 2-10-0 |

Country of origin: Germany.
Builders: Floridsdorf, Austria (No. 16626). Year: 1943.
Number of cylinders: 2 (23.6" x 25.9"). Boiler pressure: 227 psi.
Driving wheels diameter: 4' 7". Weight: 144 tons. Train brakes: Air.
Purchased from: Polish State Railways.
Current owner: Martin Haines.

The largest and considered by some to be the most impressive steam locomotive to run on the Nene Valley Railway, this locomotive was built in Austria during the Second World War, to a 1937 design, as part of the German war effort. Thousands of this type of locomotive were built for the war and they became known as 'Kriegslok', meaning 'war locomotive'.

This Kriegslok, No. 7173, was first placed in service on standard gauge lines on the Russian front between Poland and Russia (Russian railways are mostly 'broad' gauge at 4' $11^7/_8$") but any further inferences to its wartime duties are open to conjecture.

With hostilities over, from October 1950 the locomotive was allocated to Russia's South Western Railway and in October 1957 reallocated to the Odessa Railway. In April 1962 it was moved to the Belarussian Railway and was subsequently moved to Poland in 1963.

The German Class 52 is Class Ty2 in the Polish State Railways (PKP) identification system and as such, it was allocated the number Ty2-7173, which it still retains. The last duty for PKP was working heavy sand traffic in block trains in the south of Poland near Katowice.

Ty2-7173 was purchased from PKP in 1989 by Martin Haines on the condition that the locomotive had a full overhaul at one of the PKP locomotive works.

During 1990 Ty2-7173 was sent to Olesnica Works where it was completely stripped down and rebuilt before shipment to Britain. Disembarking at Felixstowe Docks, it travelled by road to the Nene Valley Railway, arriving at Wansford in ex-works condition on 20th December 1990.

A steam test took place in January 1991, but the extreme height of the locomotive unfortunately necessitated the slewing of the track under the Lynch Farm road over-bridge before the locomotive could run through to Peterborough. The Kriegslok entered service on the NVR at Easter 1991. During 1992 it was planned to change the identity of Ty2 -7173 to that of a German locomotive, Class 52, No. 52-7173.

On expiry of its boiler certificate the locomotive has been placed 'in store' in Wansford Yard sidings, pending a decision as to its future and is now (2006) for sale. However, in view of the locomotive's extreme height it would appear unlikely that, on eventual restoration, it will be able to run on any UK line other than the Nene Valley Railway.

The Kriegslok has been quoted* as an extreme example of steam locomotive wheel balancing. On each side, the centre driving wheel carries the extremely heavy big end of the connecting rod from the crosshead plus a proportion of the weight of the connecting rod driving the other wheels. To compensate as much as possible for these out-of-balance masses and to reduce the hammer-blow on the track when the locomotive is travelling at speed (which would be very considerable due to the relatively high rotational speed of the small wheels) almost half of the wheel's circular profile is taken up by balance weight (see photograph or look at the actual locomotive). All small-wheeled, 2 cylinder, heavy-haul steam locomotives travelling at speed present similar design problems, of course, but mostly to a lesser extent than the *Kriegslok*.

* Reference P.W.B. Semmens and A.J. Goldfinch: *'How the Steam Locomotive Really Works'* OUP 2000, ISBN 0 19 856536 4.

No. 52-7173 'Kriegslok' awaits a new owner at Wansford. Photo: E. Craggs

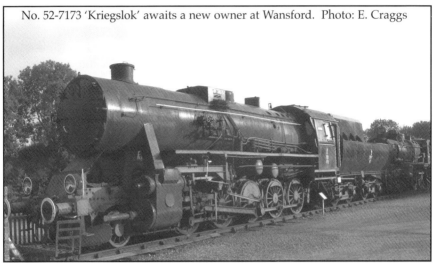

A gleaming No. 101A No. 1697
Photo: R. Maskill

Locomotive No.101A (SJ No. 1697)   Class B 4-6-0

Country of origin: Sweden.
Builders: Nydquist & Holm. No.2082. Year: 1944.
Number of cylinders: 2 (23.3" x 24.4"). Boiler pressure: 174 psi.
Driving wheels diameter: 5'9". Weight: 115 tons. Train Brakes: Air/vacuum.
Original owner: Stockholm-Westeras-Bergslagens (Sweden).
Current owner: 1697 Syndicate.

Locomotive No. 101 was the last of the three passenger locomotives built for the Stockholm-Westeras-Bergslagens Railway (SWB) to a design dating from 1909. Originally, 101 was fitted with a boiler incorporating additional superheating, but when the SWB was taken over by Swedish State Railways (SJ), 101 and its sisters were rebuilt with standard type boilers as fitted to the earlier examples of the Class. 101 was withdrawn from service in 1958 and was placed in the Swedish Military strategic reserve. Here it remained until early 1979 when it was withdrawn and sent to the scrap yard at Vislanda to be cut up. However, its arrival at the scrap yard coincided with a visit by Nene Valley Railway engineers to obtain spares for the locomotive already at Wansford.

The excellent condition of 101 was noted and a group of members, led by Mike Bratley, purchased the locomotive in July 1979. Movement of the locomotive was sponsored by shipping agents Brostrums (UK) Ltd., and 101 arrived in Peterborough on 6th October 1979. Restoration to working order quickly followed and 101 entered NVR service on 22nd December 1979.

101 has proved a popular locomotive with film makers. In the thirteenth James Bond film 'Octopussy', disguised as East German Railways (DR) locomotive No. 38.243, it successfully demolished a Mercedes saloon car in a simulated head-on crash.

Smoke deflectors, which were added for another filming contract, were eventually removed.

The locomotive now carries blue livery and its original number 101. It was withdrawn from service in February 2005 due to excessive deterioration of its firebox stays, just short of expiry of its boiler certificate and stands in Wansford Yard awaiting eventual overhaul.

Swedish No. 101A crosses Wansford Bridge with a rake of continental coaches.

Continental Main Line Steam
Locomotive No. 64.305   Class 64 2-6-2T

Country of origin: West Germany.
Builders: Krupps, Essen, No. 1308.   Year 1934.
Number of cylinders: 2 (19.7" x 26").   Boiler pressure: 203 psi.
Driving wheels diameter: 4'8".   Weight: 74.9 tons.   Train brakes: Air.
Original owner: Deutsches Bundesbahn.
Current owner: Nene Valley Railway.

64.305 is a member of one of the standard classes developed by the Deutsches Reichesbahn prior to the Second World War. Over 500 of the Class 64s were built and were used on branch lines and light suburban passenger work all over Germany.

64.305 was in the west at the partition of Germany in 1945 and remained in Deutsches Bundesbahn service until 1972. The locomotive was then purchased by a group of members of the Severn Valley Railway and moved to Bridgnorth in 1974. However it proved to be too large to be used on the SVR and was purchased by Richard Hurlock and brought to the Nene Valley Railway in August 1977.

A considerable amount of work proved to be necessary to return 64.305 to first class running order and this has been carried out at intervals over the years, culminating in a general repair during 1982-1983.

This is an ideal locomotive for operating NVR services and has seen much service on the Line. In 1985 it was sold to the Nene Valley Railway.

64.305 has featured in several TV films. The locomotive is restored in the livery and insignia of Deutsches Bundesbahn, but on occasions, in connection with filming contracts, it has reverted to the original Deutsches Reichesbahn livery.

The locomotive was taken out of traffic in 1987. In 1988, Flying Scotsman Services required an air pump to fit to 4472 *Flying Scotsman* in preparation for working the air braked stock in Australia. Consequently, 64.305's air pump was loaned to *Flying Scotsman* for its tour of Australia in 1989-90. Thus a part of this German engine really does qualify as being truly 'international'.

The locomotive now stands in Wansford Yard awaiting eventual rebuild.

The powerful shape of German Railways No. 64.305 looks impressive as it awaits its turn in the restoration line at Wansford yard.

Photo: Brian Hallett

Continental Main Line Steam
Locomotive No. 1178   Class S 2-6-2T

Country of origin: Sweden.
Builders: Motala, No. 516. Year: 1914.
Number of cylinders: 2 (19.7" x 22.8"). Boiler pressure: 174 psi.
Driving wheels diameter: 4'10". Weight: 64 tons. Train brakes: Air/vacuum.
Original owner: Swedish State Railway.
Current owner: Mike Kitchen.

1178 is representative of a class of locomotive once used widely in Sweden on branch lines and suburban passenger services .

Technically 1178 is interesting in that it retains a Schmidt superheater, the earliest type to be successfully utilised in locomotive boilers. Other interesting features include the use of front and rear carrying wheels with axle boxes supported on sliding mounts in the main frame, instead of on pony trucks or bogies as on more modern locomotives. Also, the locomotive is fitted with an acetylene lighting system fed from a cylinder mounted beneath the smokebox door, although for safety reasons this cylinder is not normally carried on the Nene Valley Railway.

In 1959, after 45 years with the State Railways, No. 1178 was withdrawn from service and placed in the Swedish Military Reserve.

The locomotive was ultimately purchased by Society member Richard Hurlock and brought to Peterborough in 1975. It was returned to steam in 1976 and in company with the Nord 4-6-0 No. 3.628, worked the Nene Valley Railway's inaugural train on 1st June 1977. No. 1178 appeared in several films and was a regular performer on NVR trains until 1992, when it was taken out of service for eventual full overhaul, pending funds and availability of 'hands'. Meanwhile, the loco. had been sold on to Mike Kitchen, the present owner.

Rebuild in Progress.

In late 2002 the decision was made to begin work on restoring the locomotive (which by now had stood in store for some 10 years) following a parallel work schedule on No. 656 *Tinkerbell* (see page 30). Dismantling work on No. 1178 began in early 2004 and by the end of June 2005 the boiler and asbestos lagging had been removed, enabling a more thorough assessment and costing of the required boiler work to be carried out.

A provisional completion target date had been set at 2006/7, so that No. 1178 (along with No. 656 *Tinkerbell*) could be put back into service as Swedish B No.101 and J94 No. 75006 ran out of their boiler 'tickets'.

However, as dismantling work on No. 1178 progressed it became apparent that a very heavy overhaul was required, with valves, pistons and motion showing more wear than had at first been anticipated. In addition, wheels would need re-tyreing and the side tanks and cab sides needed replacing and/or plating. All this, of course imposed second thoughts over the provisional return to steam in 2006/7 for this locomotive.

Nevertheless, by early 2006 the 'dismantle/rebuild race' between No. 1178 and *Tinkerbell* was described by the workshop teams as 'neck-and-neck' and widely accepted completion date is now 'a.s.a.p.'

Swedish No. 1178 awaits imminent restoration in Wansford yard.

Photo: Brian Hallett

No. 656, Tinkerbell on 27 July 1978.   Photo: Roy Harrison

Country of origin: Denmark.
Builders: Frichs, Aarhus, No. 360.   Year 1949.
Number of cylinders: 2 (16″ x 22″).   Boiler pressure: 174 psi.
Driving wheels diameter: 4′1″.   Weight: 37 tons.   Train brakes: Air.
Original owner: Danish State Railways.
Current owner: Nene Valley Railway.

No. 656 *Tinkerbell* was one of 120 such locomotives built over a 51-year span for the predecessors of the present Danish State Railways. They were based on the original design of four 'F' Class tender locomotives which had been supplied to the State Railways of Jutland-Funen, Denmark, by R and W Hawthorn of Newcastle-on-Tyne, in 1873 and which themselves, later converted to tank locomotives, remained in service until the late 1930s.

The 'adopted' version of the F Class locomotives was designed in Denmark by Otto Busse and were tank locomotives from the outset. The old Hawthorn design was closely followed, but in place of the Stephenson *inside* valve gear fitted to the Hawthorn machines Busse adopted the Trick-Allan straight-link *outside* valve gear. Although long since superseded in British practice, this had been simultaneously developed by Herr Trick, Head of German Railway Engineering (and under whom Busse had been apprenticed), and by Alexander Allan, Chief Engineer, London and North Western Railway, both in the 1850s - when the original Nene Valley Railway from LNWR Blisworth to Peterborough was still in its first 15 years. Although similar to the Stephenson valve gear the Trick-Allan gear uses a straight expansion link and moves the link and die block at the same time.

Between 1898 and 1923, 105 Busse-designed 'F' locomotives were built for the Danish Railways - 51 were built in Denmark itself, whilst a further 15 were built in Italy, 33 in Germany and 6 in Belgium.

These Busse Class F's earned a reputation for being durable and amenable to operate.

The Class F's main duties, apart from light goods train and passenger working on secondary lines, was the shunting of passenger carriages and goods wagons onto and off the many Danish ferries linking the mainland and island railheads along the deeply indented Danish coastline.

The 656 Story.
Following the devastation of the Second World War, there was an urgent need by Danish State Railways for shunting locomotives. Once again Busse's long-established 'F' design was called upon and a further 15 such locomotives - including No. 656 - were built in Denmark in 1949 by Frichs, Aarhus (the same locomotive works, incidentally, that in the following year was to build the Danish 4-6-2 Class 'E' locomotive No. 996, currently at the Railworld Centre). These post-war 'F' Class locomotives were still built basically to Busse's original drawings, but were fitted with stronger buffers and buffer beams and larger coal bunkers. They are alleged to have cost 105,000 Danish kroner each, equivalent to £5,500 in 1949 money, to manufacture. Of the 120 Class 'F' locomotives built, 13 remain extant, the oldest being an 1899

Italian-built locomotive and of these it is believed that about 6 are in working order, No. 656 being one of them.

During it's DSB working life Locomotive No. 656 was allocated to Nyborg, Hensel Fredericia and Esbjerg Depots. Although no specific record of its work duties appears to have come to light, it is reasonable to assume that No. 656 continued in the 'traditional' Danish 'F' role of shunting, light goods and passenger train working and with the remaining railway ferry duties (numerous railway bridges having replaced many of the earlier ferries), before being withdrawn from regular service and placed in store at Aarhus Depot.

To the Nene Valley Railway.

From Aarhus, No. 656 was purchased privately, for around 17,000 kroner and transported to Peterborough in 1975.

The locomotive was steamed for the first time on the Railway in 1976 and after the formal opening of the Nene Valley Railway in 1977 saw regular use on the lighter off-peak trains. As the locomotive is fitted with a bell, it became affectionately known by NVR members as 'Tinkerbell'.

Like all Danish locomotives No. 656 carries the colours of the Danish flag around its chimney. Its antique appearance has made it a favourite with film makers and it has appeared in several sequences including one in 'Secret Army' where the locomotive and its train were 'shot up' by an RAF Mosquito aircraft.

In 1985 656's owner, Richard Hurlock, sold the locomotive (along with Norwegian coach No. 601) to John Snasdell, but Locomotive No. 656 was taken out of traffic in 1986 with a failed firebox and placed in store (where it was to remain for some 16 years) pending availability of resources for a complete rebuild.

In 2003 John Snasdell generously donated Norwegian Coach No. 601 to NVR, followed by No. 656 Tinkerbell in 2004.

Rebuild in Progress.

In late 2002 the decision was taken by the NVR Board to bring the locomotive back into service and to follow a parallel dismantle/rebuild schedule along with Swedish 2-6-2T No. 1178 (see page 28).

Systematic dismantling work began on No. 656 in the winter of 2003/4 and by the summer of 2005 the boiler and asbestos lagging had been removed, revealing the extent of the boiler work required. Dismantling continued through 2005. Some of the spring hanger and brake rigging pins had long since seized and needed considerable tonnage to remove them. Most of the mechanical parts, including the cylinder bores were found to be in reasonable condition, apart from the coupling rod and other journals which were found to be worn and in need of replacement.

The copper firebox was bulged and cracked and was originally condemned as being 'beyond economical repair', resulting in the locomotive's early withdrawal from service in 1986. However, it is anticipated that modern copper welding technology will enable the firebox to be re-worked back to serviceable condition. The ash pan is badly corroded and a new one will need to be made.

Dismantling No. 656 was complete by the end of 2005. It had been discovered during dismantling that on its previous overhaul (in its pre-NVR days) 656's injector feed pipes (normally concealed by the water tank panels) had been incorrectly assembled, preventing water being drawn from the full tank depth. This appears to explain the loco's reputation for rapidly running short of water and is raising expectations of operational improvements when the machine is brought back in service. By early 2006 the dismantle/rebuild 'competition' between *Tinkerbell* and Swedish No. 1178 was gathering momentum (Denmark - v - Sweden!) and reported to be 'neck-and-neck'. But the anticipated 2006/7 'back to steam' has been amended to a.s.a.p. and as this book goes to press we are keeping our fingers crossed.

The above account of the background and story of No. 656 *Tinkerbell*, has been compiled almost exclusively from a thoroughly-researched and detailed account of the 'F' Class locomotives, by David Withers, published in Nene Steam No. 80, Winter 2005/6, to which readers are referred for further information.

No. 656 Tinkerbell in Wansford workshop. Photo: Roy Harrison.

Nord Pacific No. 3.628 .   Photo: Roy Harrison.

Continental Main Line Steam
Locomotive No. 3.628   Class 3500 4-6-0 Compound

Country of origin: France.
Builders: Henschell & Company, Germany, No. 10745. Year: 1911.
Number of cylinders: 4 (2 High pressure, 15″ x 25.2″ and
           2 Low pressure, 25.5″ x 25.2″). Boiler pressure: 229 psi.
Driving wheels diameter: 5′9″. Weight: 113 tons. Train brakes: Air.
Original owner: Nord Chemin de Fer.
Current owner: Chris Randall.

No. 3.628 was built to the design of M. du Bousquet for the Nord Railway of France and incorporates the compound expansion principles of M. du Glehn.

Until the advent of the Class E Pacifics No. 3.628 and her sisters handled the heavy expresses from the Channel Ports and Belgium to Paris. Despite their comparatively modest dimensions these locomotives could develop in excess of 2,000 hp. On nationalisation of the French Railways in 1938 No. 3.628 became SNCF No. 230D116 and was fitted with a le Maitre multiple-jet blast pipe and chimney. The locomotive was damaged by the RAF during the Second World War and ended her career on semi-fast and freight trains in the mid 1960s, having covered over 2 million miles.

No. 3.628 was purchased in 1972 by the Nord Locomotive Preservation Group and moved to Ashford, Kent, for restoration. In 1975, with its original number restored, No. 3.628 came to the Nene Valley Railway and in company with 2-6-2T No. 1178, worked NVR's inaugural train on 1st June 1977.

In 1980 No. 3.628 was offered for sale by the NLPG and because of its technical importance was purchased by the Science Museum for the National Collection.

In 1983 its new owners commissioned Resco (Railways) Ltd of Woolwich, to carry out a cosmetic overhaul, which was completed in 1984 when No. 3.628 returned to Wansford. In 1985, as part of GW150 celebrations it visited Didcot Railway Centre. It was taken out of traffic in 1988 after spending 10 years in service and now stands on display in Wansford Yard.

No. 3.628 awaits restoration in Wansford Yard.
Photo: Gordon Kobish

33

Continental Main Line Steam
Locomotive No. TKp 5485   Class T2D   (SLASK) 0-8-0T

Country of origin: Poland.
Builders: Chrzarnow Locomotive Works. Year: 1959.
Number of cylinders: 2 (21.6" x 21.6"). Boiler pressure: 200 psi.
Driving wheels diameter: 3'7". Weight: 60 tons. Train brakes: Air.
Maximum Tractive Effort: 28,000 lbf. Maximum Speed: 25 mph.
Original owner: Polish State Railways.
Current owner: Martin Bell.

Developed by the Polish Chrzarnow Locomotive Works in co-operation with Henschell & Sohn of Kassel, this class of powerful shunting locomotive, T2D (SLASK), was introduced in 1950 during the post-war period of industrial growth in Poland.

This rugged locomotive is claimed to be capable of hauling a train weighing 3,200 tons at speeds of up to 10 mph. Its maximum speed is 25 mph and it is able to negotiate 325 ft radius curves due to the second and fourth axles being of floating design.

The locomotive is fitted with a substantial superheated boiler and seamless steel tubes. The steel fire box has welded stays and is fitted with a rocking grate and an ashpan that can be emptied by the fireman from the footplate.

Heusinger sliding valve gear is used, lubricated by a Friedmann's lubricator, common on Polish designed locomotives.

Lighting is provided by a 24 volt steam generator. Production of this locomotive class ceased in 1960. By this time 390 had been built, being widely used throughout industrial Poland, including oil-fired versions to be found in that country's oil refineries. 90 T2Ds had been exported to the Chinese People's Republic.

The 'TKp' designation is from the Polish system: T - Freight, K - Tank engine and p denoting 0-8-0 wheel arrangement. There were no other known variations in the designation for this class of locomotives as they were all built as industrial shunters only.

This locomotive, TKp 5485, worked at collieries in southern Poland before being sold to the Meldigen Museum in Belgium. The locomotive was then purchased privately and was moved to Llangollen in 1998, where it received an extensive overhaul in the railway workshops there. On completion of this work it came to the Nene Valley Railway, arriving by road on 12th September 2001.

No. 5485 worked its first NVR passenger train on 1st December 2001 and sees frequent use on NVR services, although it has required fitter's attention to numerous boiler and mechanical problems and further remedial work is anticipated. In spite of this and in spite of being a 'low speed' machine, the locomotive has earned a reputation of being easily capable of keeping to NVR's working timetable.

Locomotive No. 5485's potential of being able to haul heavy trains at low speeds, continuously, due to its small wheels, large boiler and high steaming capacity (analogous with a crawler tractor in the world of construction machinery) is not put to the test on NVR's relatively level heritage line.

Polish tank locomotive No. 5485 prepares to haul its next train during 2005.
Photo: Robert Maskill.

Tram Locomotive No. 1626 'Toby' after arrival in Wansford car park.
Photo: Roy Harrison.

Continental Main Line Steam Locomotive No. 1626	'Toby'	0-4-0 VBT

Country of Origin: Belgium.
Builders: Cockerill. Year: c. 1890.
Number of cylinders: 2 (19" x 28"). Boiler pressure: 140 psi.
Driving wheels diameter: 2'7$\frac{1}{2}$". Weight: 17 tons. Train brakes: Air.
Original owner: Charles Focquet et Cle, Etterbeck, Vilvoorde.
Current owner: Mrs. Pauline Hall.

In 1835 Société John Cockerill, of Seraing, Belgium, built the first steam locomotive to run on the European Continent. The Company has been building railway locomotives ever since. Eventually becoming Cockerill Mechanical Industries SA (CMI) and from December 1982 an independent subsidiary of Cockerill, Sambre, CMI now employs more than 2,000 people, with shunting locomotives listed amongst its current products.

In 1987 several Cockerill-built tram locomotives were discovered at Vilvoorde, Brussels. As one of *Thomas'* friends is a tram engine called *Toby*, members decided that one of these engines would be ideal to rebuild to a similar design to GER G15, the design on which *Toby the Tram Engine* is based, with suitable modifications incorporated to reflect current practices.

The late Graham Hall and the late Dr. George Cree purchased Tram No. 1626 from Brussels and it arrived at NVR, Wansford by road on 22nd December 1987.

The tram was completely stripped down and is to be rebuilt with larger frames, complete with cow-catchers and side skirts, plus a wooden body, based upon the design once familiar on the Wisbech and Upwell Tramway in the neighbouring County of Norfolk.

It is a matter of great sadness to the members of NVR that Graham Hall and George Cree will never see the project achieve fruition.

However, work on *Toby's* restoration continues, albeit very slowly, but the current challenge centres around the tram engine's boiler which, it is estimated, requires funding in the region of £4,000 - £5,000.

Work progress on 'Toby' in Wansford shed at the time of writing.

Photo: Brian Hallett.

<table>
British Main Line Diesel
Class 14 (Type 1) 0-6-0 Diesel Hydraulic Locomotive Nos. D9516, D9518, D9520 & D9523
</table>

Country of origin: United Kingdom.
Builders: British Rail, Swindon. Year: 1964/65.
Engine: Paxman Ventura 6YJXL 650 hp @ 1500 rev/min. Tractive effort: 32,000 lbs.
Transmission: Voith/North British L21 7U Hydraulic unit/Hunslet 650 gear box.
Locomotive weight: 50 tons.
Driving wheels diameter: 4'0".
Train brakes, D9516, D9520 & D9523: Air/Vacuum. D9518: Vacuum only.
Original owner: British Railways (WR). For current owners see below.

Background to the Type 1's (Class 14's) .

56 of these Type 1 diesel hydraulic locomotives (it was initially envisaged that there would be over 300), numbered D9500 to D9555, were built in 1964/65 by British Railways' Swindon Works, as the final stage of the Western Region's diesel hydraulic programme. At this time the other British Railways Regions had adopted diesel - electric traction to replace steam.

The Type 1s, principally designed to replace the numerous 'Pannier' and 'Prairie' tank engines on the Western Region, were built for the South Wales coal fields and for short freight 'trip' workings (hence the 4-character route indicators), where periodic shunting around a station yard would be required between fast dashes along the main line. But even as the locomotives were being built, much of this work was rapidly disappearing as the so-called 'Beeching Axe' reshaped British Railways and closed down wayside stations, along with their wagon load goods traffic and indeed, some of the main lines themselves.

Initial allocations of the Type 1s were therefore on the Western Region, at London's Old Oak Common (Shed Code 81A), Bristol Bath Road (82A), Worcester (85A), Cardiff Canton (86A) and Landore (87E). The locomotives became surplus as their work disappeared and many were stored at places such as Gloucester and Worcester, although a number had been transferred to Hull Dairycoates (50B) for use on the North Eastern Region, ousting the remaining steam locomotives in that area.

With hindsight, it can now be seen that the Type 1s need never have been built and in fact, all the locomotives had been withdrawn from BR service by 1970, less than 5 years from new.

It would have been at this time that, under BR's new TOPS classification, the Type 1s were re-classified as Class 14s.

From Main Line to Industrial.

Realising the economic advantages of acquiring cheap, relatively new, ex BR locomotives, Corby based Stewart & Lloyd Minerals Ltd. (subsequently part of the British Steel Corporation) purchased 23 Class 14s from BR in 1968. These were allocated to S & L Minerals' ironstone quarries at Buckminster and Harlaxton in Lincolnshire and to Corby and Glendon in Northamptonshire, replacing their existing steam fleet. At about the same time the National Coal Board purchased 19 Class 14s from BR, allocating many of them to the Northumberland area. This 'bulk purchase' of Type 1s/ Class 14s by S & L Minerals and the National Coal Board included the 4 locomotives currently on the Nene Valley Railway.

With the subsequent contraction of the British steel industry and closure of the quarries and then Corby Steelworks itself in 1980 (where the remaining members of BSC's fleet had gathered) the locomotives were, once again, surplus to requirements and were either scrapped, re-sold or acquired for preservation. The decline of the British coal industry followed within a few short years and the same fate befell the NCB Class 14s.

Into Preservation.

As a consequence of this short locomotive-class story, the Four Class 1s based on the Nene Valley Railway have almost parallel histories:-

D9516 was supplied new to Cardiff Canton Depot, South Wales, in October 1964. It was then transferred to Landore, Swansea in May 1965 and finally to Hull Dairycoates in December 1966 where it was withdrawn from BR service. The locomotive was purchased by Stewarts and Lloyds Minerals in November 1968, where it was re-designated No. 56. In October 1981 it transferred to its current owner, Gerald Boden, at the Great Central Railway and finally moved to the Nene Valley Railway in November 1988.

D9516 is dual braked so is able to operate with vacuum and air-braked rolling stock. It is currently painted in its original two-tone BR green and sees regular use on NVR services.

D9518 emerged from Swindon Works at the end of October 1964. It was allocated new to Cardiff Canton, remaining with this depot throughout its short working life on BR. D9518 was amongst the last handful of the class in BR service, (all the remaining working survivors being withdrawn on 26th April 1969) having been placed in store twelve days previously.

D9518 was sold to the National Coal Board, Northumberland Area, in July 1969 and was transferred by rail from Cardiff Canton to Ashington Colliery. At Ashington, the loco became No. 7 (Plant No. 9312/95) and was repainted in the distinctive NCB Ashington blue livery, a lighter shade of blue than the standard NCB blue. In this location, the locomotive worked a fairly uneventful life hauling coal and spoil trains around the extensive Ashington system which took in Ashington, Woodhorn, Ellington and Lynemouth Collieries, with occasional visits to Lambton Engine Works, Philadelphia for overhauls and repairs (in 1975 and 1980). Its last overhaul had been completed in 1986 and it was considered to be one of the best locos in service on the system. Its engine subsequently developed an oil leak and was removed from the locomotive to be rectified. Unfortunately, the Miners' Strike then intervened and the engine was neither rectified nor refitted to the locomotive.

With the run down of the British coal industry and the subsequent closure of the Ashington Colliery system, all of the remaining nine NCB Class 14s were sold for preservation. NCB D9518/No. 7 was transferred by road to the Rutland Railway Museum, Cottesmore, arriving there on 26th September 1987. Here it remained as a static exhibit and in 2006 was transferred to the care of the Iron & Steel Traction Group, based at NVR Wansford, although the locomotive remained at Cottesmore. It is however expected to be transferred to Wansford during late 2006.

D9518 remains in its National Coal Board livery, in contradistinction to the usual instant return to BR livery - frequently the 'fate' of ex-BR diesels 'salvaged' from industry for preservation. In fact D9518 had only spent $3^1/2$ years in BR livery, then 17 years in NCB Ashington blue. Although a spare power unit has been acquired, No. 7 currently remains as a 'spares back-up' to other working members of the class, the need to restore the loco to working order not being justified due to the availability of other working examples.

D9520 was completed at Swindon Works on 11th November 1964 and initially allocated to Cardiff Canton. In January 1967, it was transferred to Hull (Dairycoates) with other members of the Class for work in the North East Region but was withdrawn from BR service there in April 1968.

Purchased by Stewart & Lloyds Minerals Ltd. the loco arrived, in company with D9523 (see below) at Glendon Quarries near Kettering on 16th December 1968 where it became No. 24 (Plant No. 8311/24) and was used to haul wagons of ironstone from the quarries to the exchange sidings, from where BR then hauled the trains to Corby Iron and Steel Works.

A year later, on 12th January 1970, the loco travelled along the Midland Main Line to Gretton Brook loco depot for work on the Corby Ironstone Quarries system, where it was eventually renumbered 45 in the Minerals' loco fleet. In the course of time, it became the designated loco on the North Bank crusher sidings where all incoming ironstone was received by Corby Steelworks and as such, the loco would often work around the clock on a three shift system.

With the decline in steel production nationally and the subsequent closure of Corby's ironstone quarries and the Iron and Steel Works in 1980, No. 45 was transferred to the Corby Tubeworks (which is still in operation today) for short-lived general shunting and transfer duties.

On 16th March 1981, the loco (along with '61' - D9529 - see below) left Corby Works in a BR freight train bound for preservation on the North Yorkshire Moors Railway (NYMR). However, with the influx of larger diesels on the 'Moors Line', D9520 was again surplus to requirements and was re-sold, moving south, this time by road, to Rutland Railway Museum, Cottesmore, thus returning to the East Midlands old ironstone field (but United Steel Corporation's old 'territory') on 21st February 1984. In March 1998, the loco was transferred on loan to Nottingham Transport Heritage Centre at Ruddington. It was no stranger to the Great Central main line - the loco had previously been a guest at GCR, Loughborough's Diesel Gala in October 1985 to celebrate the Twenty-First Anniversary of the Class, working with the GCR's then resident Class 14s, D9516, D9523 and D9529 - the latter having also 'moved on' from the NYMR.

On 20th April 2004, D9520, now owned by the Iron and Steel Traction Group, arrived at Wansford for completion of restoration and is now permanently based on the Nene Valley Railway, being 'reunited' with D9516, D9518 and D9523.

The detailed restoration programme, currently being undertaken by its owners, the IST Group, covers mechanical overhaul and rewiring and an internal and external repaint - which will show the loco's original BR two tone livery as D9520 and its Corby Quarries identity of '45'. To enable D9520/45 to operate air braked trains (as built, the loco was vacuum braked only) an air braking system has been installed.

D9523 was supplied new to Old Oak Common in December 1964. It was transferred to Bristol Bath Road in October 1965 and finally to Hull Dairycoates in January 1967.

On withdrawal by BR, D9523 was moved to Stewarts and Lloyds Minerals, Glendon Quarries, along with D9520 (see above), on 16th December 1968.

D9523 was transferred to the Great Central Railway and its present owner, Gerald Boden, in October 1981 and finally moved to the Nene Valley Railway in June 1989. D9523 is painted maroon and sees regular use on NVR services. The locomotive is dual braked, so as with D9516, it can work with vacuum and air-braked rolling stock.

D9516 BR Class 14 arrives at Orton Mere in March 2001.
Photo: David Harrison.

No. 9523 looking resplendent in its maroon livery.   Photo: Brian Hallett

Class 31 (formerly Brush Type 2)
Locomotive No. 31 271   A1A-A1A Diesel Electric

Country of origin: United Kingdom
Builders: Brush Traction Ltd, Loughborough. Year: 1961.
Engine: English Electric 12SVT 1,470 hp @ 850 rev/min.
Maximum tractive effort: 35,900 lb
Transmission: Brush TG160-48, 823 kW dc generator with individual traction motors on outer axles of each bogie.
Locomotive weight: 107 tons.
Driving wheels diameter: 3'7". Locomotive brakes: Air/vacuum.
Maximum speed: 90 mph.
Original owner: British Railways Eastern Region.
Current owner: A1A Locomotives Ltd.

Class 31s - Background.
There can be no other class of British main line diesel locomotive more deserving of a place on the Nene Valley Railway than the Brush Type 2, for it was these locomotives that formed the diesel contribution of the 50-50 steam/diesel passenger services in the last days of the Northampton-Peterborough Line. Mostly fitted with headcode boxes the east-bound workings were designated the code 2E67 and westbound 2M67. When the line closed as a through route it was the Brush Type 2s that continued to work the remaining freight services between Peterborough and Oundle and the last workings from Nassington Ironstone Quarries.

The Type 2s were developed from an existing Brush design for an order for 25, 1,000 hp main line diesel locomotives supplied to the Ceylon Government Railway in 1951/52. (Ceylon became Sri Lanka in 1972). The first batch of 20 Type 2s for British Railways left the 'Falcon' Works, Loughborough, in late 1957 (the numbering being D5500 to D5519) and by the time their production ceased in October 1962, 263 had been built.

Each weighing 104 tons, the locomotives were originally powered by Mirrlees JVS12T turbocharged, 4-stroke, V-12 engines, producing 1,250 hp @ 850 rev/min. The starting tractive effort (with 26% adhesion) was 42,000 lb and maximum speed was 80 mph.

As with most main line diesel locomotives the engine is started by motoring the main generator from batteries slung underneath the main frame. Several engines were subsequently uprated to 1,365 hp and the maximum speed of these locomotives increased to 90 mph. However, the Mirrlees engines eventually developed a fatigue cracking problem in the main casing and the entire class of locomotives' were progressively re-engined with English Electric 12SVT 1,470 hp units, thus uprating the locomotives' specification to that shown at the head of this section.

With the introduction of British Rail's TOPS classification in 1968, the re-engined units became Class 31s and the still-Mirrlees powered locomotives became Class 30s, although the fitting of the new engines ensured that none ever carried numbers in the Class 30 series.

The first 20 Type 2s were fitted with an electro-magnetic control system but this was replaced by electro-pneumatic equipment in the production series.

Provision was thus made from the outset for the locomotives to operate in multiples of two or three together if required, under the control of a single front end driver. For this reason the characteristic 'flat' cab ends incorporated a door for corridor connection between locomotives. However, this provision was rarely used by British Railways and only served to produce draughts in the cab. The doors were eventually sealed up as the locomotives were refurbished at Doncaster Works in the late 1970s.

Class 31 - 31271* (See page 43 for photographs)

This locomotive was originally numbered D5801 and entered British Railways service at Stratford Depot, East London, on 8th June 1961. With the introduction of BR's TOPS classification in 1968, when re-engined Type 2s were re-classified as Class 31s, D5801 became 31 271. The locomotive was variously allocated to eight Eastern Region and two Midland Region locomotive sheds during its main line career, Toton being its final home. Here it was 'stored unserviceable' from 1st May 1977, its final passenger working having been the 'Multiple Marauder' Rail Tour from Kensington Olympia to Crewe, paired with 31 308, on 10th August 1996.

The locomotive was subsequently purchased by A1A Locomotives Ltd. and moved to the Midland Railway, Butterley by road on 28th May 1998.

At that time A1A Locomotives were fully occupied rebuilding classmate 31 108 from scrap condition and '271' was purchased solely as a source of spare parts; indeed progress with 31 108 was helped by the fitting of six cylinder heads removed from 31 271 and overhauled.

31 108 was out shopped in June 2000 and made an extended visit to the Nene Valley Railway between September 2001 and May 2005. In 2001 A1A Locomotives decided to begin restoring 31 271 to full working order, initially to prevent valuable components deteriorating. During its thorough 'top end' mechanical rebuild, three cylinder liners were found to be scored as a result of broken piston rings. These liners were renewed and all pistons were machined prior to being fitted with new rings and re-installation in the engine block. A considerable programme of electrical work was also undertaken.

The locomotive worked its inaugural services at Butterley on 20th April 2002. Extensive bodywork repairs were undertaken between January and May 2004, when undercover accommodation became available in the Matthew Kirtley Building at Swanwick Junction and the locomotive was repainted into Trainload Construction livery as carried in its closing period of main line service.

31 271 was formally named 'Stratford 1840-2001' by John Watling, President of the Great Eastern Society, at the National Railway Museum's 'Railfest 200' event on 31st May 2004. The naming is a tribute to Stratford's rich locomotive history and in particular, its central role in the Class 31 story. Whilst 31 271 itself spent its first year in traffic as a Stratford loco, (it was also based there between November - December 1988 and March 1989 - October 1990) no less than 75% of the Class were allocated there at some time during their BR careers.

In addition to participating in NRM's 2004 Railfest 200, the rebuilt 31 271 has also visited the Mid Hants., the East Lancs., the Keighley and Worth Valley and the West Somerset Railways, prior to arriving at the Nene Valley Railway. The NVR Class 31 locomotive exchange took place on 11th May 2005, when A1A Locomotives' 31 108 departed for its original Butterley base, after a stay of almost three and a half years on the NVR, whilst 31 271 arrived to take its place on NVR services.

Both Class 31 locomotives' rail movements, via the Fletton Loop, took place courtesy GB Railfreight and Network Rail. 31 271 took part in the Nene Valley Railway's Autumn Diesel Gala on 17th - 18th September 2005.

With the entire Class 31s being allocated to the Eastern Region when new, it is quite possible that 31 271 (as D5801) could have worked over the Nene Valley Line right through to Northampton and even after 1964 (when the Northampton Line closed) on freight duties between Peterborough and Oundle or on ironstone traffic from Nassington Quarries to Peterborough and beyond. Wansford Station was then closed - these were the pre-NVR days - so 31 271 would have run through Wansford Station non-stop and with passenger trains at least, considerably faster than it is permitted to run today. Perhaps one day some photographic evidence of such runs will come to light!

*The above record of 31 271 is based upon an account written for the NVR Stock Book by Steve Harvey, Publicity Director, A1A Locomotives Ltd.

No. 31 271 awaits departure from Wansford.
Photo:
   Brian Hallett.

No. 31 108 in 'Railfreight' livery
Photo:
   Robert Maskill.

British Main Line Diesel
Locomotive No. D306 *'Atlantic Conveyor'* Class 40 (Type 4) 1Co - Co1 Diesel Electric

Country of origin: United Kingdom.
Builders: Robert Stephenson & Hawthorn, Darlington. (E2726/RSH8136).
Year: 1960. Engine: English Electric 16SVT Mk11 (2,000 hp @ 850 rev/min).
Tractive effort: 52,000 lb. Transmission: 6 x English Electric EE526/5D traction motors (one on each of the three inner axles of each bogie).
Locomotive weight: 133 tons. Driving wheels diameter: 3'9". Max. speed: 90 mph.
Train brakes: Vacuum.
Original owner: British Railways (LM Region).
Current owner: Gerald Boden.

In the British Railways Modernisation Plan of 1955 English Electric received an order for ten Type C, 2,000 hp locomotives (later designated Type 4) . The first, D200, was delivered in 1958, entering traffic on the Great Eastern lines of the Eastern Region. All ten of the 'pilot batch' were allocated to either the East Coast or the Great Eastern main lines.

The trials were successful and a further batch of 190 locomotives was ordered from English Electric Vulcan Foundry. Due to the production Deltics then being built by English Electric, assembly of 20 of the Type 4s, including D306, was carried out at Robert Stephenson & Hawthorn, Darlington, D306 being completed in October 1960.

D306 spent most of its time shedded in the London Midland Region, being initially allocated to Crewe for running in, followed by Liverpool Edge Hill, Willesden, Crewe again, then London Midland Western Lines. In the early 1970s BR introduced the TOPS computerised data system. Under this the English Electric Type 4s became Class 40s and D306 was renumbered 40106. Although the fleet was being repainted in corporate blue around this time, 40106 remained green, the colour favoured by enthusiasts and even when she was overhauled at Crewe Works in 1978 BR decided to keep 40106 green. The locomotive was now allocated to Manchester Longsite Depot and its 'special' green livery became popular for rail tour duties.

The locomotive was withdrawn by BR in 1983 due to being vacuum braked only. It was purchased by the present owner in the spring of 1984 and moved to the Great Central Railway. On 11th August 1984 it was named *Atlantic Conveyor* in remembrance of the container ship of that name that was sunk in the Falklands Campaign.

In 1988 during a repaint to original 1960 condition, D306 was renumbered D326 and given split head-code boxes to star in the film 'Buster', based on the Great Train Robbery.

In February 1990, D306 was moved by road to Wansford and immediately entered service on NVR. Since arriving D306 has visited Rail Open days at various national locations.

During 2005 the locomotive was fitted with a new set of batteries and has received attention to parts of its bodywork which were showing signs of corrosion. Nevertheless, D306 is in full working order and can be seen in regular service on the Nene Valley Railway.

Class 40 D306, "Atlantic Conveyor" on freight duty at Wansford.

Photo: Brian Hallett

Class 56 56 057 shines in the sun at Wansford shed during 2005.

Photo: Robert Maskill

Class 56 (Brush Type 5) Locomotive No. 56057

Co-Co Diesel Electric
'British Fuels'

Country of Origin: United Kingdom.
Builders: British Rail Engineering, Doncaster. Year: 1979.
Engine: Ruston-Paxman 16RK3CT, V16. Cylinders: 10" bore x 12" stroke, 4-stroke with a compression ratio of 7:1. Twin camshaft. Napier turbocharger developing 3,250 bhp @ 900 rev/min.
Started by two Bosch 110 volt dc starter motors.
Capacities: Lubrication oil: 120 gal. (SAE 30); Engine Coolant: 308 gal. Diesel fuel: 1,150 gal.
Transmission: Main alternator: Brush BA1101A.
Traction Motors: 6 x Brush TM73-62 dc motors mounted one on each axle.
Driving wheels diameter: 45". Pneumatic sanding equipment.
Locomotive maximum speed: 80 mph.
Locomotive weight: 126 tons. Maximum tractive effort: 61,800 lbf.
Fitted for multiple working via a 27-point connector. Not fitted with train heating equipment.
Original owner: British Rail, Eastern Region. Current owner: Privately owned.

The Class 56 Story.
The concept of the Class 56, British Rail's first high-powered heavy-haul diesel electric freight locomotives, came into being in the early 1970s. The need was identified for a single locomotive that could handle freight trains weighing in excess of 1,500 tons, at speeds up to 75 mph; a departure from the long-standing design specification that had applied to mixed traffic locomotives such as the Class 40s and 47s.

The outcome was the award of a contract to Brush Traction of Loughborough for the construction of a first batch of locomotives, in conjunction with the State-owned Electroputere Company of Craiova, Romania, who had experience of building high powered freight locomotives for the Eastern bloc.

The adopted design was a development from the original 1960s Brush 4,000 hp *Kestrel* diesel electric locomotive which had subsequently been sold to Russian State Railways in 1971. Its then unusual design feature was its innovative ac-dc electrical transmission, which was incorporated into the Class 56 design and has since been widely adopted in locomotives built subsequently.

Of the 135 Class 56 locomotives eventually built between 1976 and 1984, the first 30 were built at the Craiova, Romania, works. The first two of these locomotives, Nos 56001 and 56002, arrived in the UK via the Harwich train ferry on 4th August 1976 and on 7th August were hauled through the eastern counties by a Brush Type 2, en route to inspection and acceptance testing by British Rail. Manufacturing defects were found on the first and subsequently, other, Romanian built locomotives and certain components of the Romanian 'CP2' bogie assemblies had to be reworked at Brush's Loughborough Works. It was not until February 1977 that the first locomotive, 56001, was accepted into service on British Rail.

The last Romanian built Class 56 was observed, ex Harwich, being hauled through Stowmarket on 14th September 1977.

Meanwhile, an order for 30 Class 56s (which included 56057) had been placed with British Rail Engineering Ltd., to be built at Doncaster. However, the manufacture of certain sub-units was undertaken by other BREL plants. Roofs, fuel tanks and cab frames were made at Ashford; cab desks at Eastleigh and radiator housings were manufactured at Swindon. All the UK built Class 56s were fitted with Romanian bogie assemblies. The first of the Doncaster built Class 56s, No. 56 031, was accepted into BR service in mid-May 1977, three months after acceptance of the first Romanian locomotive.

A further 55 of the class were eventually built at BREL, Doncaster and a further 20, the final batch, were built at BREL Crewe, from where the very last Class 56 locomotive to be built entered BR service in November 1984.

The Class 56s were fitted with cab-to-shore radio telephones, slow speed control - down to half a mile per hour for merry-go-round train loading and unloading and all were equipped for multiple working. However, they were not fitted with head code boxes as the use of head codes had by then been phased out. An unattractive square ventilator grill on the front of the cab earned these locomotives the nickname 'grids'.

The body shell of the Class 56s was a development of the earlier Brush Type 4s (later designated Class 47s), incorporating a sophisticated 'pre-stressed skin' design, in which the bodywork sides of the locomotive add to its strength and take a share of the weight carrying and traction and braking forces instead of the more conventional practice of relying solely on the strength of the base frame. This approach was adopted to improve the strength - weight ratio of the locomotives. The triangular box-section 'skeleton' of the body box-construction can just be seen when the ambient lighting catches the sheet metal work appropriately.

In spite of design shortcomings and manufacturing and maintenance cost implications, the Class 56s proved themselves to be heavy haulers. Capable of exerting a continuous tractive effort of 52,700 lbf against that of their most powerful Class 47 predecessors' 30,000 lbf, it became commonplace for Class 56s to haul 1500 ton coal trains between the Yorkshire and the Midlands collieries to the Aire and Trent Valley power stations, with ample power in reserve, whilst the Class 47s were frequently limited to 1150 tons. The Class 56s were also to be seen working 1400 ton stone traffic trains (37 high capacity hopper wagons) from the Yeoman Mendips quarries to Acton Yards, a duty which had hitherto required two Class 47s. It was reported that the 2700 tons iron ore trains running from Port Talbot Harbour to Llanwern Steel Works, the heaviest regular BR freight working, had required three Class 37s but were displaced by Class 56s working in pairs.

Class 56 freight working ceased in early 2004, although several have (in early 2006) been brought back into service in the UK and some remain at work in Continental Europe. But to all intents and purposes Class 56s have been superseded on Network Rail tracks first by the UK built Class 58s, then 59s, 60s and 66s - the latter classes being designed and built entirely on the North American Continent. So although the Class 56 locomotives were the first of the British-built heavy-haul diesel electric locomotives, they were, at the same time, signalling the end of an era of British locomotive building.

The 56057 *British Fuels* Story.

Against the background of the Class 56 story outlined above, NVR's No. 56057 was built at BREL's Doncaster Works and completed in March 1979, being amongst the last of the first batch of 30 Class 56s built at Doncaster. A British-built locomotive with Romanian bogies.

The locomotive was initially allocated to Toton (Nottingham) from where it would have been used for MGR coal trains and other heavy freight work originating in the area. The locomotive was recorded as being used on MGR workings from the Nottinghamshire/Derbyshire collieries to Didcot Power Station, on which runs it would have easily handled 1,500 ton trains.

The locomotive transferred through various depots including Bristol and Cardiff, returning to Toton on several occasions. In September or October 1992, 56 057 is on record as having stood in for a failed Class 158 DMU on the 06:48 Birmingham to Cambridge/Stansted Airport cross-country passenger service and return. A sledge hammer - nut job!

With the privatisation of British Rail in 1993, ownership of 56057 passed to English, Welsh & Scottish Railways (EW&S) and was the second locomotive to carry the new EW&S livery. On 27th June 1996, 56057 was named *British Fuels* at Aberdeen, in recognition of its association with that industry.

The locomotive continued in its regular freight duties almost to the turn of the Century, but with changes in the patterns of freight workings, the take-over of freight duties by the more developed UK-built Class 58 locomotives and from 1998, the Canadian-built GM Class 66s, by 1999, 56057 had been placed in store at Immingham Depot where it was to remain for some four years..

The locomotive was acquired by its present owner, for preservation, on 16th June 2004 and was moved to the Nene Valley Railway in July 2004. As such, 56057 was the first Class 56 to be placed in preservation on a heritage railway. A great deal of refurbishment work has been carried out by the present owner and in the evening of August 26th 2004 the locomotive made its first test run on NVR metals hauling a rake of NVR Continental coaches.

Still in its EW&S livery, the locomotive made its first public appearance at NVR's three day Autumn Diesel Gala in October 2004, the first Class 56 to haul a passenger train on a heritage railway. The locomotive has since been repainted in BR 'large logo' blue and sees regular use on NVR trains.

56057 is not the heaviest (at 126 tons it is about the same weight as No. 73050 *City of Peterborough*), but it is the most powerful and hardest pulling locomotive on the NVR and its Romanian connections make it a fitting addition to the Nene Valley Railway as an international railway.

In EW&S livery, Class 56 057 departs Orton Mere. Photo: Robert Maskill.

British Industrial Diesel
Locomotive No. 11   *'Birch Coppice'*   4w Diesel Hydraulic

Country of origin: Un ited Kingdom.
Builders: Sentinel/Thomas Hill (134C).   Rebuilt as a diesel in 1964.
Engine: Rolls-Royce 8 cylinder supercharged C8SFL, 311 bhp.
Transmission: Rolls-Royce, incorporating torque converter and Self Changing Gears Ltd. 8.4:1 final drive.   Driving wheels diameter: 3'2".
Locomotive weight: 36 tons.   Maximum tractive effort: 22,000 lb.
Original owner: National Coal Board.   Current owner: Gerald Boden.

This 24'4" long, 4 - wheeled diesel locomotive started life as a steam engine. After Sentinel ceased steam locomotive production in 1958 Thomas Hill built their works near Rotherham to repair and rebuild Sentinel steam locomotives as diesels.

No. 11 TH134C is a 36 ton rebuild using the frame of a 200 hp 4 wheeled Sentinel vertical boilered steam locomotive, retaining chain drive to the wheels. Its diesel engine, incidently, is the same basic unit as fitted in the Rolls-Royce Sentinel 0-6-0 diesel hydraulic locomotive No. 22, DL 83 - see page 56 in this book and also in the 0-4-0 Sentinel Barbabel - see page 58 in this book.

The locomotive was in service at several NCB sites, finishing its working life at Birch Coppice Colliery, Tamworth, Staffordshire. It was purchased in full working order by Gerald Boden and moved to the Great Central Railway in October 1980. Such was the condition and power of the locomotive that for two years it was the Permanent Way Dept. Loco, assisting with the moving and laying of 2 $^1/_2$ miles of track from Rothley to Leicester North.

No. 11 moved, with *Mayflower,* to HLPG, Hull in 1989 and both locomotives then came to NVR Wansford in May 1991.

No. 11, Birch Coppice on shunting duties at Wansford.   Photo: Brian Hallett.

British Industrial Diesel
Class 438A 0-4-0
Locomotive No. D1123   *'Muriel'*   Diesel Hydraulic

Country of origin: United Kingdom.
Builders: English Electric, Newton-Le-Willows. Year: 1966.
Engine: Cummins NHRS 6B1, supercharged, 305 bhp.
Transmission: British Twin Disc with torque converter, series 10000. Self Changing Gears Ltd. RF11 final drive.
Driving wheels diameter: 3'4". Maximum locomotive speed: 18 mph.
Locomotive weight: 34 tons. Maximum tractive effort: 20,000 lb.
Original owner: Newalls Insulation Company.
Current owner: Nene Valley Railway.

Newalls Insulation Co. of Washington, County Durham ordered two shunting loco-motives from English Electric Co. Ltd., which were delivered in 1966. Named after the Company Director's daughters, they bore the names *Muriel* (1123) and *Margaret*.

     Both locomotives were subsequently purchased in 1968 by the British Sugar Corporation, Wissington, Norfolk, where they worked until made redundant in 1982. They were both then moved to the BSC plant at Peterborough, but as there were no available duties for 1123 this locomotive was sold to the Nene Valley Railway, arriving at Wansford in 1983.

     Muriel is the only Cummins-powered locomotive on the NVR. Originating in the USA, the Cummins Engine Co. was a relatively late entrant to the UK rail trac-tion market, opening up their Shotts, Lanarkshire, production plant in the late 1950s. Even then, Cummins diesels were only slowly adopted for UK rail traction. So *Muriel,* with its now-obsolete *supercharged* power unit, is a 'rare' heritage locomotive.

No. D1123 at Wansford.   Photo: B. Hallett

British Industrial Diesel
Locomotive No. D2654   *'Doncaster'*   0-4-0 Diesel Electric

Country of origin: United Kingdom.
Builders: Yorkshire Engine Company, Sheffield.   Year: 1957.
Engine: Rolls-Royce C6TFL, 250 bhp @ 1,800 rev/min.
Transmission: Electric, single British Thomson Houston traction motor.
Driving wheels diameter: 3'4".   Locomotive maximum speed: 20 mph.
Locomotive weight: 30 tons. Maximum tractive effort: 18,000 lb.
Original owner: Pilkington Brothers Ltd.
Current owner: The Yorkshire Engine Group.

This locomotive was built by the Yorkshire Engine Company in 1957, as one of an order for five locomotives for Pilkington Brothers Ltd., glass manufacturers of St. Helens, Merseyside.

These locomotives, with their original 200 bhp Rolls-Royce C6SFL super-charged diesel engines and a tractive effort of 18,000 lbf., performed sterling service for Pilkingtons until 1984, when a new plant at St. Helens rendered *Doncaster* and her sister locomotives redundant.

Doncaster was duly sold, for a nominal sum, to the Doncaster and District Railway Preservation Society. However, problems with locomotive accommodation at Sandtoft led to the machine then being sold to the Yorkshire Engine Group and transferred to the Nene Valley Railway.

Since arriving at Wansford the locomotive has been completely rebuilt, incorporating the higher rated Rolls-Royce C6TFL turbocharged engine. It is used as required in Wansford Yard.

Photo: R. Maskill

British Industrial Diesel Locomotive No. 2896	'Frank'	4 Wheeled Diesel Mechanical

Country of origin: United Kingdom.
Builder: F. Hibberd and Sons Ltd. Year: 1944
Engine: Perkins D3.152: 35 bhp
Locomotive weight: 5 tons
Original owner: BOCM (Silcocks) Ltd., Selby, Yorkshire.
Current owner: Nene Valley Railway.

This locomotive was purchased by Peterborough Railway Society in 1972 and was at that time powered by a Dorman 25 hp, 2 cylinder petrol engine dating from 1913. The Apprentice School at Perkins Engines Ltd., Peterborough, carried out a complete overhaul of the machine. This work included the fitting of a modern diesel engine, a 25 kva generator and a 35 cfm, 100 psi air compressor, as well as a more comfortable cab and new bodywork, all this work being completed in 1976.

The locomotive saw light duty on the Nene Valley Railway until suffering a broken buffer beam and was subsequently taken out of service.

In the spring of 2006 work began on *Frank* to bring it back into service, using parts, including the buffer beam, from No. 2894 *Percy*, a brother 4 wheeled Hibberd locomotive, also of 1944 vintage, which has also stood out of use at Wansford and will now be scrapped once the work on *Frank* is complete.

Planet Locomotive No. 2896 "Frank".   Photo: Brian Pearce.

'Stanton No. 50' Janus Class 0-6-0 Diesel Electric

Country of origin: United Kingdom.
Builders: Yorkshire Engine Company, Sheffield. Year: 1958.
Engines: 2 x Rolls-Royce C6SFL supercharged units, totalling 440 bhp @ 1,500 rev/min.
Driving wheels diameter: 3'6". Locomotive maximum speed: 23 mph.
Locomotive weight: 48 tons. Maximum tractive effort: 32,000 lb.
Original owner: Stanton Ironworks Company.
Current owner: Privately owned within the Iron & Steel Traction Group.

Background.
This machine is an example of what is generally acknowledged to be one of the most successful industrial locomotives of its type ever built.

The Yorkshire Engine Company, formerly of Meadow Hall Works, Sheffield, was a long established and well respected steam locomotive builder with numerous industrial and main line locomotives to its credit, built during the nineteenth and twentieth centuries. The Company was taken over by the United Steel Companies Ltd. in 1945, primarily to build up and standardise the locomotive fleets of the USC's various steelworks, coal and coke works and ironstone quarries, with large numbers of locomotives being supplied to Scunthorpe, Rotherham, Stocksbridge (Sheffield) and Workington.

The Yorkshire Engine Company produced its first diesel locomotive in 1949, with the first 'Janus' type being built in 1956. The design - so named after the mythical Roman god who, with two faces, looked both ways - found immense popularity with a wide range of industrial railway operators, especially the steelworks, due to the rugged simplicity of operation and maintenance. The 48 ton, 0-6-0 diesel-electric, centre cab machine was highly regarded in particular by drivers and maintenance staff.

Powered by two Rolls-Royce 6-cylinder, supercharged diesel engines*, (see page 54) together producing 440 bhp. the locomotive can be operated on either or both engines according to the power required.

The Yorkshire Engine Company closed down in 1965, the last locomotive to be built being a 'Janus' type and by that time just over 100 'Janus' machines had been produced. Some are still at work seeing daily use in industrial service throughout Great Britain, particularly at the Corus steelworks at Scunthorpe, North Lincolnshire; a fitting tribute to a fine design.

Stanton No. 50.
The Nene Valley Railway 'Janus' locomotive, originally *Stanton No. 50*, was completed at Meadow Hall Works on 30th September 1958, with Works No. 2670 and was delivered to the Stanton Ironworks Company's Ilkeston (Derbyshire) iron and steel making complex near Nottingham.

With nationalisation of the UK steel industry in 1967, Stanton became part of the British Steel Corporation. In 1973 *Stanton No. 50* was transferred to BSC's coke ovens at Brookhouse near Sheffield and then, in 1981, to Orgreave Coke Works, Sheffield. By this time the locomotive had been renumbered 2444/20. On closure of

Orgreave Works, in August 1990, the loco, which was nominally in working order, was presented to Appleby Frodingham Railway Preservation Society and moved, on loan to Rutland Railway Museum, Cottesmore.

It was later purchased by the late Chris Jones and moved to the Nene Valley Railway on 26th July 1993, where the Yorkshire Engine Group commenced restoration, including the fitting of re-tyred wheels and side rods, which had been preserved with the loco from Orgreave Works.

The locomotive has more recently been purchased by members of the Iron and Steel Traction Group and restoration work continues in Wansford Workshops. The two Rolls-Royce engines are basically in reasonable condition, requiring only relatively minor external attention. The electrical power and control equipment, however, is badly deteriorated due to the passing of time and is to be rewired to current standards, using trunking and conduit, which did not feature in the machine's original build. Train air and vacuum braking equipment is to be installed. Notwithstanding these essential 'modifications', every effort is being made to restore the locomotive as authentically as possible to its original condition. Replacement name plates are being obtained and the loco is being restored in its original Stanton Ironworks Co livery indicating its original identity - 'Stanton No. 50'.

*Each of the 'Janus' Class Rolls-Royce C6SFL *supercharged* engines is a similar basic engine to the RR C6TFL *turbocharged* unit used in the Yorkshire Engine Company's NVR 0-4-0 locomotive No. 2654 *Doncaster* - see page 51.

Stanton No. 50 at work.   Photo: Gordon Kobish

British Industrial Diesel
Locomotive No. D2969 Class DY5 0-4-0 Diesel-Mechanical

Country of origin: United Kingdom.
Builders: Ruston & Hornsby, Lincoln (304469). Year: 1951.
Engine: Ruston 6VPH, 165 bhp. Transmission: Ruston, mechanical gearbox.
Driving wheels diameter: $3'2^{1}/2''$. Maximum locomotive speed: 15 mph.
Locomotive Weight: 28 tons. Maximum tractive effort: 14,350 lb.
Original owner: British Sugar Corporation, Spalding, Lincs.
Current owner: Roy Harrison.

This locomotive was delivered new to the British Sugar Corporation, Spalding Sugar
Beet Factory in 1951, where it worked the internal sidings until 1984, when rail
traffic into the Spalding factory ceased. The locomotive was transferred on loan to
the Nene Valley Railway, where in 1988 it became the Wansford Yard shunter, replacing Ruston 321734 which had failed.

British Sugar plc released the loco as surplus and it was purchased by Roy
Harrison in 1992, when restoration work began.

The owner has decided to restore the locomotive to BR condition like sister
locos D2957 and D2958 which were scrapped.

Class DY5 No. D2969 at work.   Photo: Roy Harrison.

Country of origin: United Kingdom.
Builders: Rolls-Royce, Shrewsbury (Works No. 10271). Year: 1967.
Engine: Rolls-Royce C8SFL, supercharged, 325 bhp @ 1,800 rev/min.
Transmission: British Twin Disc, torque converter, CF11500.
Self Changing Gears Ltd., RF11 final drive.
Driving wheels diameter: 3'4". Maximum locomotive speed: 17 mph.
Locomotive weight: 48 tons. Maximum tractive effort: 28,800 lb.
Train brakes: Air/vacuum.
Original owner: Hired to Stewart & Lloyd Minerals Ltd., Corby, from Rolls-Royce.
Current owner: Privately owned within the Iron and Steel Traction Group.

Early Days.
This locomotive was delivered to Stewart & Lloyd Minerals Ltd., Corby, in October 1967 on a loan basis while Rolls-Royce plant developed and built the proposed 'Steelmen' locomotives. Given works No. 10271 the locomotive became Stewarts & Lloyds' *No. 22.*

However, with the nationalisation of the UK steel industry, the 'Steelmen' contract was cancelled by Stewart & Lloyds Minerals, which itself became part of the British Steel Corporation. Locomotive No. 22 remained with British Steel at Corby, but was rarely used.

In June 1971 No. 22 was sold to London Transport, travelling over BR lines to London under its own power. It was allocated to Lillie Bridge Depot for ballast train working and carried London Transport No. DL83. It was subsequently modified with low-level couplings and the fitting of a 'tender' by removing the rear buffers. It remained in service with London Transport until a failure in May 1989, which resulted in its withdrawal from service. In March 1994 the locomotive was offered for sale.

DL83 was purchased by a private NVR member and arrived at Wansford on 14th July 1994. The locomotive has since been restored to full working order, including the fitting of both air and vacuum braking systems. Its diesel engine, the Rolls-Royce 8-cylinder, supercharged, C8SFL, is the same basic unit as fitted in locomotive No. 11, *Birch Coppice.* See page 49.

Torque Converter Modification.
Sentinel DL83 has recently undergone an interesting transmission modification. The locomotive's torque converter was, from new, designed to be driven and lubricated by circulating diesel fuel drawn from and returned to the locomotive's diesel fuel tank, rather than the more conventional separate hydraulic transmission fluid circuitry. Using *diesel fuel* as the transmission medium in this way was common practice in certain torque converter transmissions built in the 1950s and 60s and served to simplify the 'plumbing' of machinery so designed. This system appears to have worked satisfactorily for many years. However, with the more recent removal of sulphur from diesel fuel, there is concern that this 'cleaner' fluid may not provide adequate lubrication, particularly for ball and roller races and that it may cause

damage to the carbon seals such as those fitted in certain torque converters.

As a consequence, during 2002, locomotive DL83 was modified to allow its transmission to operate on conventional transmission fluid. This involved the manufacture and fitting of a new 24 litre hydraulic tank, which was very conveniently able to be fitted on the right hand running plate, behind the side sheet and adjacent to the cab. Other work included rearranging the hydraulic piping and ancillaries and of course isolating the engine's fuel system from that of the torque converter.

To date, the locomotive is reported to be operating satisfactorily, with the transmission appearing to run more smoothly than before, hopefully giving a longer life expectation to this 40-year old 'early modern' locomotive.

This kind of work may not belong to the age of steam, but it is one more example of the wider scope of work in which heritage railways are becoming involved. NVR currently has three other locomotives which use diesel fuel in their torque converters - D1123 *'Muriel'*, No. 11 *'Birch Coppice'* and *'Barabel'*.

Sentinel No. DL 83 in Wansford Yard.   Photo: Robert Maskill

Rolls-Royce 'Sentinel' 'Barabel' 0-4-0 Diesel Hydraulic

Country of origin: United Kingdom.
Builders: Rolls-Royce, Shrewsbury (Works No. 10202). Year: 1964.
Engine: Rolls-Royce C8SFL, supercharged, 325 bhp @ 1,800 rev/min.
Transmission: British Twin Disc, torque converter, CF11500.
Self Changing Gears Ltd. RF11 final drive.
Driving wheels diameter: 3'4". Maximum locomotive speed: 21 mph.
Locomotive weight: 31 tons. Maximum tractive effort: 24,200 lb.
Train brakes: Air.
Original owner: Oxfordshire Ironstone Company Ltd.
Current owner: Privately owned within the Iron and Steel Traction Group.

Background.

Although *Barabel* is an 0-4-0 locomotive, an interesting comparison can be made with No. 22, NVR's 0-6-0 Sentinel, described on the previous page. But first, the story of *Barabel* begins in the Oxfordshire ironstone field ...

The Oxfordshire Ironstone Company (OIC) had begun its quarrying operations in 1917, a few miles to the west of Banbury to tap the massive reserves of ironstone in that area. Over the years there had been some 33 standard gauge steam locomotives working in that system. 15 were at work in the early 1960s when the decision was made to dieselise the whole system, using new 0-4-0 Rolls-Royce Sentinel locomotives. Although these 0-4-0 Sentinels were fitted with the same Rolls-Royce supercharged engines and nominally the same torque converter and transmission as the 0-6-0 design to which No. 22 belongs, *Barabel* is some 17 tons or 35% lighter than the 0-6-0 design* (see page 59). No. 22s maximum speed is quoted as 17 mph whereas the lighter weight *Barabel's* maximum speed is 21 mph, although *Barabel* could not be expected to pull the same weight of train at that speed.

The Oxfordshire Ironstone Company initially acquired two 0-4-0 Sentinels in 1961 and 1962 and these worked alongside the steam locomotives. A further eleven 0-4-0 Sentinels were ordered, built in one series and delivered by rail at regular intervals from Shrewsbury to Banbury, between September 1964 and July 1965. Of the OIC fleet of thirteen 0-4-0 Sentinels, eight, of which *Barabel* was one, were of the 'light-weight' design, described above, for hauling loaded wagons from the quarry face to the ore crusher at Wroxton. The remainder were heavier, 40 ton* versions of the 0-4-0s, for OIC's 'main line' working from Wroxton to the BR main line exchange sidings $1^{1}/2$ miles north of Banbury station. With the unexpectedly rapid decline of the UK ironstone industry the Oxfordshire Ironstone Company's system closed in September 1967, less than three years after the new Sentinels had begun work. So the company's entire fleet of almost-new 0-4-0 Rolls-Royce Sentinels became redundant.

Barabel's Story.

Works No. 10202, *Barabel* was delivered from Shrewsbury to the Oxfordshire Ironstone Company by rail on 29th December 1964, the sixth delivery of the fleet within the second 'quarry' batch of five locos weighing 31 tons. The 'Barabel' nameplates were transferred from the original steam locomotive (Hudswell Clarke 0-4-0

ST Works No. 1868, built in 1953) to the new Sentinel 10202, being named after the wife of Mr. A.G. Stewart, Chairman of the Oxfordshire Ironstone Company 1945 - 1951 and Chairman of parent company, Stewarts and Lloyds Ltd., 1945 - 1964.

With the run-down of the Oxfordshire Ironstone Company's quarries *Barabel* was the first of the Sentinels to be declared redundant and was transferred to Stewarts & Lloyds' Bromford Tube Works, Erdington, Birmingham on 17th July 1967 where it was to remain for the next 27 years.

During its life at Bromford Works *Barabel* underwent various modifications, receiving some parts from a similar but older Sentinel No. 69 (Works No. 10099, built in 1962), also based at Bromford. *Barabel's* original engine compartment sliding door arrangement was replaced by the lighter-weight panelling still in place today, easing maintenance access and the original distinctive side sheets were replaced by hand rails.

The locomotive lost its nameplates and old identity and its superb OIC crimson lined out black and yellow livery, with red buffer beams, to be repainted the ubiquitous 'industrial' yellow with 'wasp' stripe ends. At a later stage *Barabel* received its present royal blue paintwork with black and yellow 'wasp' stripes on the buffer beams and sides below the running plates.

By December 1994 *Barabel* had been sold on from Bromford Works and eventually ended up at the Round Oak Rail Terminal at Brierley Hill, West Midlands, where it was fitted with train air braking equipment to enable it to handle air braked main line freight wagons of steel. This steel terminal, which eventually became Innovative Logistics, was on the site of part of the former Round Oak Steel Works which itself had been supplied with ironstone from the Oxfordshire Ironstone Company all those years before!

To the Nene Valley Railway.

Barabel was acquired for preservation by members of the Iron & Steel Traction Group and moved to the Nene Valley Railway on 15/16th March 2006. In working order and with its former identity reinstated - albeit with temporary 'nameplates' - apart from maintenance and servicing, the loco has been immediately made available for general yard shunting duties at Wansford.

Within the Iron & Steel Traction Group work programme *Barabel* will eventually be fully restored to its 'as built' condition with bonnet doors and distinctive side sheets reinstated. Whilst the loco was never vacuum fitted at OIC, it is intended that a vacuum brake system will be installed, whilst retaining the locomotive's existing air braking system.

As a fitting tribute to the Oxfordshire Ironstone Company and its fine diesel fleet, *Barabel* will be restored to its original crimson livery, lined out with yellow and black and with red buffer beams.

* Although the additional pair of wheels and associated components, together with the longer chassis, would make the Sentinel 0-6-0 locomotives heavier than the 0-4-0 versions, both machines have the same basic deck machinery. The different weights (ranging from 30 to 50 tons) of the various versions of these locomotives, to give the wheel - rail adhesion required, were obtained by varying the ballast weighting of each machine, i.e. the thickness of the end 'buffer' plates and/or the addition or removal of ballast blocks within each locomotive's structure.

Sentinel No. 10202 'Barabel', in Wansford yard.　　Photo: Robert Maskill.

Wansford Shed with a considerable variety of locomotives
and rolling stock on view.　　Photo:　Robert Maskill

Passenger Coaching Stock - Introduction

The Nene Valley Railway's collection of passenger coaches is every bit as varied as the locomotives. The following pages give details of British and Continental passenger coaches, from the lightest at 30 tons to the heaviest at over 55 tons.

British.

Beginning with the more mundane there are examples of LMS and LNER coaches, both of which are currently being restored to their original pre-grouping internal decor and liveries. Then there are some 16 British Railways 'Mk. 1' coaches of four different types, some of which are in regular use on NVR trains, whilst others are awaiting or undergoing refurbishment or restoration. There is one British Rail 'Mk. 2e' coach, although this is permanently out of service as a running vehicle, but is in daily use as a sales/exhibition coach in Wansford station.

Not to be forgotten is the three-car diesel multiple-unit set, not so long ago regarded as 'modern', but now classified as 'Heritage' stock. This is used regularly on off-peak and other services.

Continental.

There are 14 Continental passenger coaches on the Nene Valley Railway with examples from Belgium, Denmark, France, Italy and Norway. They are, in their own way, representative of different traditions in design and craftsmanship and present a sharp contrast alongside British passenger coaches. It is these coaches, together with NVR's Continental locomotives, that have made the Nene Valley Railway unique in the UK as an *International* heritage railway. NVR's bridges, tunnel, platform clearances and double-track sections comply with the 'Berne' Loading Gauge and can accommodate the extra width and height of these Continental rail vehicles, in regular use on timetabled services.

Some of the Continental coaches are characterised by their tapered body ends which maintain clearance between 'nose and tail' swing-over and line-side structures on the outside of track curves.

Pride of place amongst the Continental coaches must go to the two Wagon-Lits vehicles, which have seen service in most countries in Western Europe. For many years *Compagnie Internationale des Wagon-Lits et due Tourisme* was responsible for the provision of dining and sleeping cars on International trains throughout Europe. To provide these services CIWLT developed a series of elegant and comfortable vehicles which set standards which other companies followed.

The two Wagon-Lits vehicles on the NVR are representative of the Company's inter-war designs and similar vehicles can still occasionally be found, although in ever decreasing numbers in service in Europe.

When travelling on the NVR in any of these Continental coaches, or even just sitting in them, it doesn't take much imagination to visualise the extremes of everyday human dramas these coaches must have witnessed over the years, against the changing landscapes of Continental Europe, from Norway to Italy or East Germany to Spain.

The Nene Valley Railway coaching collection is growing all the time and it is our aim to include as wide a selection of passenger vehicles as opportunity and finances allow.

British Pre-Nationalisation Passenger Coaching Stock

LNER Third Corridor (TK) No. 61634.
LNER Group Vehicle

Built 1926, Stratford, to Diagram 25.

This coach was the first in a batch of thirteen built to a length of 52' 6" instead of the normal 61' 6", for use in East Anglia. Originally built with seven compartments and two toilets, it was rebuilt in 1963 for departmental use and numbered ADE320904. It was used at Hull Dairycoates shed with their steam crane. It was later moved to Hull Botanic Gardens Motive Power Department as a mess van, until being finally withdrawn in 1978.

After withdrawal it was acquired by the Hull Locomotive Preservation Group and was more recently purchased by Gerald Boden and moved to Wansford in 1991. It is now owned by Gordon Maslin. The coach is to be restored to its former LNER teak finish.

LNER No. 61634 under wraps prior to restoration in Wansford Workshops.

Right: One of the LNER design bogies removed for overhaul.

LMS Brake Composite Corridor (BCK) No. 18017
LMS Group Vehicle

Built 1927 at Wolverton.

Lot No. 320 to Diagram 1755.

This coach is believed to have been built for a part of the Royal Train. In 1933, under the LMS coach renumbering scheme, it received the new number 6678. In 1960 British Railways converted it for the Regional Mechanical and Electrical Engineer (RM&EE), for which it was given the identity number ADM395758. Under this guise it was purchased by S. Bywaters and brought to Wansford, where it has been restored to LMS livery. It is now owned by Gary Walker.

LMS Brake Composite Corridor (BCK) Coach No. 18017 (6678), before restoration.
Photo: David Harrison.

British Nationalised Passenger Coaching Stock
British Railways Mk. 1 Vehicles

In the 1950s the newly formed British Railways wished to standardise its rolling stock. As with all BR stock the design featured the best of the 'Big Four' railway companies. The Mk. 1 coaches, built between 1951 and 1963, mostly resemble those of the LMS main line stock and are of all steel construction. The Mk. 1 coach bodies are 64' 6" long and 9' 0" wide and mostly weigh 32.5 tons. Coach lighting is 24 volt from lead-acid batteries charged by an under-floor dynamo, belt-driven from an axle pulley. Inside, the vehicles are arranged in various configurations, these being Open, Corridor, Brake, Sleeper, Restaurant/Buffet in either First or Second Class or both as a Composite. Parcels traffic wasn't neglected, with BG and GUVs being on 57' 0" frames, as was the Suburban Compartment stock.

The vehicles in the NVR collection are of four different Second Class designs. It is hoped to acquire more in the future.

A selection of these coaches is in general use as the main NVR passenger stock, with a selection of the Continental stock in use at other times.

Some of these ex-BR coaches are used as support vehicles for the various NVR work groups. Some coaches are being restored into authentic liveries to form an accurate representation of main line railway travel in Britain in an earlier era.

Number	Type	Builder	Year Built	Lot No.	Weight Tons	Bogie Type
1872 (1)	RMB	BR Wolverton	1962	30702	38	C
4200 (2)	TSO	BR York	1956	30172	33	BR1
4466 (8)	TSO	Birmingham Rly C & W Co.	1957	30226	33	BR1
4627	TSO	BR York	1957	30203	31	B4
4635 (3)	TSO	BR York	1957	30203	33	BR1
4686	TSO	BR York	1957	30375	33	BR1
4794 (7)	SO	BR York	1957	30376	33	BR1
4919	SK	BR Wolverton	1961	30690	37	C
24997	SK	BR Derby	1956	30208	33	BR1
25347 (4)	SK	BR Wolverton	1957	30349	34	BR1
25639	SK	BR Wolverton	1958	30428	34	BR1
26193	BSK	BR York	1962	30726	36	C
34935 (5)	BSK	Metro-Cammell, Saltley	1956	30229	34	BR1
35043	BSK	Gloucester Rly. C&W Co.	1956	30233	35	BR1
35239 (6)	BSK	BR Wolverton	1958	30427	35	BR1
35248	TSO	BR Wolverton	1958	30427	33	B4

Coach Types:

TSO - Tourist Second Open. 64 second class seats. 2 toilets.

Continued on page 81 ...

Swedish Class B, No. 101 outside Wansford Shed. This picture shows the contrast between different countries' design ideas compared with the British B1 Class shown below.   Photo: Robert Maskill

No. 1306 'Mayflower' gleaming in the sunshine before hauling the 'Rail Mail' train in June 2006.   Photo: Edwin Craggs

Class 5, No. 73050 City of Peterborough at Orton Mere. Taken before the nameplates were fitted. Photo: Robert Maskill

The sturdy profile of Polish tank Class T2D No. TKp 5485 is shown to advantage in this picture by Robert Maskill.

German Class 64, No. 64.305 awaits restoration in the Wansford Yard siding.
Photo: Robert Maskill

This massive German 'Kreigslok' No. 52-7173 waits forlornly for a new owner and hopefully restoration, in the Wansford Yard siding.   Photo: Edwin Craggs

Swedish Class S No. 1178 awaits its future in the Wansford Yard siding.
Photo: Robert Maskill

French Class 3500, No. 3.628 Compound at Wansford in 1988.   Photo: D. Harrison.

No. 75006 looking smart as it awaits its next duty at Wansford.

Photo: Robert Maskill

No. 1800, now known to everyone as the original 'Thomas'. Named by the Reverend Awdry, author of the famous 'Thomas' children's books.

Photo: Edwin Craggs

D 306 'Atlantic Conveyor' out in the Cambridgeshire countryside through which the NVR passes.   Photo: Robert Maskill

Sentinel No. DL83 gleams in Wansford yard.   Photo: Robert Maskill

Class 56 No. 56 057 awaits departure time with Class 31 No. 31 271 on the same train as the bottom picture.　　　　　　　　　　　　　Photo: Robert Maskill

Class 31 (31 162) No. 5580 and Class 40 D306 at Peterborough. March 2000.
Photo: David Harrison.

Class 14 No. 9516 in Wansford Yard.   Photo: Brian Hallett

Class 14 No. D9523 looking immaculate at Wansford.   Photo: Robert Maskill

No. 66 706 "Nene Valley" GBRf Class 66 on its 'Naming Special' departing Wansford 25th April 2003.

Photo: David Harrison.

Class 117 3-car DMU on a Peterborough NV service at Ferry Meadows.

Photo: Robert Maskill

Visiting Locomotives to NVR

Black Five No. 45337 with continental coaches in December 2004.

Photo: Robert Maskill

Visiting Class 66 No. 66558 during 2005 Diesel Gala.

Photo: Robert Maskill

Belgian No. 21013
in Wansford Yard

Belgian No. 42170 in
the Continental rake.

Belgian No. 21033
at Wansford

**Photographs by
Brian Hallett and
Robert Maskill.**

Danish No 477 at
Wansford.

Wagon-Lits No.
2975 at Wansford

BR Mk 1 (SK) No. 25639 at Wansford.

BR Mk 1 (BSK) No. 35248 at Wansford

BR Mk 1 (BSK) No.34935 at Wansford.

BR Mk1 (SO) No. 4794 'Christabel'

LMS (BG) No. 30976

Norwegian teak bodied No. 601

**Photographs by
Brian Hallett,
Robert Maskill
and
Edwin Craggs**

BR Mk 1 (TSO) No. 4919 in special NVR livery.

French, Nord No. 7122. An early integral body design.

BR Mk 1 (BSK) No. 35239 almost finished after overhaul at Wansford.

BR 21T Hopper No. B431752

LMS CCT No. 37071

31T Plate No. 460411

Brake Van No. B954024

31T 'Hi Shock' No. B721890

Pal Van No. 778810

Centre wagon is BR Van Fit No. B761651

SR 12T 5 Plank Open No. 5869

LNWR 8 Plank No. 143288

BR 25T Lowmac No. B904523

BR Trout Ballast Hopper No. DB992164

BR Van Fit No. B785122

DSB No. TG8959

BR Van Fit No. B771300

BR Mackerel Ballast Hopper No. DB992358

BR CCT No. DB94796

SR Brake No. 55550

LMS Tank Wagon No. 1914

COUPLINGS - EVERY VEHICLE HAS ONE AT EACH END

Screw-link type coupling found on most locomotives and some coaches.

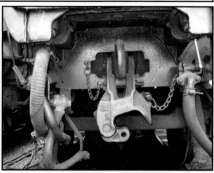

A Buckeye coupling in the lowered position. Notice the 'jaws'.

The same coupling raised with jaws closed as seen above right.
Photos: E.Craggs.

The jaws are open ready to couple to another vehicle. When the two couplings connect the jaws lock closed.

Wansford Signal Box looking west.

The Signal Box - an essential part of any railway operation. Photo: R. Maskill

...continued from P64.

RMB	Restaurant Miniature Buffet. 44 Second Class Seats. RMB Buffet counter and store. 2 toilets.

SK   Second Corridor.   48 Second Class seats.   2 toilets.

BSK   Brake Second Compartment.   Brake compartment & parcels area.
24 Second Class seats in compartments.   1 toilet.

SO   Second Open.   48 Second Class seats.   2 toilets.

Bogie Types:

BR1   Standard double bolster leaf spring bogie. Maximum speed: 90 mph.
Weight: 6.1 tons.

C   Commonwealth. Heavy cast steel, coil spring bogie.
Maximum speed: 100 mph.   Weight: 6.75 tons.

B4   Coil spring, fabricated bogie. Maximum speed: 100 mph.   Weight: 5.2 tons.

Notes:

1.   Originally air braked and electrically heated and used in Southern Electric Multiple Units.

2.   *'Britannia Bar'*. 32 seats and 1 toilet removed to provide space for bar area and store. 8 seats repositioned in bar area. (40SIL)

3.   Bogies and seats originally removed and the carriage body used to provide office accommodation at NVR Wansford. With the opening of the new station building this coach became a museum vehicle.

4.   Originally preserved at Alresford in 1982 and later at Pitsford. This coach was one of the only batch of SK vehicles to be fitted with a *single* bolster leaf spring bogie (weighing 5.3 tons).

5.   Owned by Gerald Boden for use with No. 1306, *Mayflower* and D306 *Atlantic Conveyor* when on UK main line duties. Originally allocated to the Southern Region and had 32 Second Class seats and a periscope fitted for the guard.

6.   *'Greene King'*. Owned by Nene Valley Railway. A thorough restoration of this vehicle including its bar, now named *'The Karl Mayes Bar'*, in memory of the late Karl Mayes who worked as a volunteer in NVR's Carriage Dept. Completed in early 2006.

7.   Bought in 1987 for use as a restaurant at the "Railway Inn" Whittlesea, until it was acquired by the NVR in 2000 and painted into "Pullman" style livery named and "Christabel".   At the moment it is not fitted with train brakes which restricts it to Wansford. Normally used on Platform 5 for extra covered seating.

8.   Originally preserved in 1986 by the Scottish Railway Preservation Society (SRPS) at Falkirk, being 'plated' to run on BR as SCR99816. In 1986 the vehicle was moved to Perth then to Bo'ness in 1991. Sold in 2005 and moved to Wansford, arriving on 31st October 2005.

BR Mk 1 CONTRASTS

NVR Mk 1 coach rake departs Orton Mere for Peterborough on 17 June 2006. Nearest camera SK No. 25639.

Items in this picture are: 25639 SK; 25347 SK; 35239 BSK; 35248 BSK; 4919 TSO; E70294E TPO; 34935 BSK; & D306 Class 40 locomotive.

BR Mk1 BSK No. 35248 at Wansford January 2001.

BR Mk1 TSO NO. 4919 in maroon at Wansford in January 2000.

Mk1 BSK No. 35248 at Wansford in February 2000.

Photographs on this page by David Harrison.

British Nationalised Passenger Coaching Stock
British Rail Mk. 2e First Open (FO) No. 3227

Built in Derby in 1972, Lot No. 30843, this coach was fitted with 48 First Class seats in 2 + 1 layout and 2 toilets. Stones air conditioning and B4 bogies were fitted from new. The coach was allocated to the London Midland Region until 1983, when coaches were transferred to depots, M3227 then being allocated to Oxley (OY). By 1986 it had been transferred to Old Oak Common (OM).

In 1988 'sectorisation' came into being, stock being allocated to pools and 3227 slotted to IWRX (Inter City Western Region). In 1989 this changed to ICHX (Inter City Charter Unit). In 1990 3227 was re-allocated to Euston (EN) IWCX (Inter City West Coast). It returned to Old Oak Common in Pool ICHV (Inter City Charter VIP) in 1992 and finally moved to Bounds Green (BN) in 1994.

3227 was sold to Watermans' Railway Empire in 1995 as part of the Special Trains Unit privatisation. In early 1997 it was acquired by London Weekend Television for a filming assignment on the NVR, for the TV drama 'London's Burning'. 3227 arrived at Orton Mere on 14th February 1997, along with two other vehicles, 17023 (MK. 1 BFK) and 2833 (Mk. 1 BCK), behind EWS Class 37 locomotive No. 37427. The latter two coaches eventually returned to Bounds Green.

In true TV style 3227 caught fire and was saved by the Blackwall Firefighters. The interior was stripped for filming, so when LWT's work was complete NVR bought it for a home for the Model Railway. As the B4 bogies were in working order and the coach itself was to be 'stuffed and mounted' a pair of scrap 'Commonwealth' bogies were substituted.

3227 is now situated in the Exhibition Platform 4 at Wansford Station, painted in Southern Region green.

Partly sheeted during roof repairs, No. 3227 at Wansford.   Photo: E. Craggs

Diesel Multiple Unit
Class 117 Diesel - Mechanical Three Car Set

Country of Origin: United Kingdom.
Builders: Pressed Steel Ltd., Swindon. Built: 1960.
Car Types and Numbering designation: Driving Motor Brake Second (DMBS)
No. 51347.
(Un-powered) Trailer Composite Lavatory
(TCL): No. 59508.
Driving Motor Second (DMS): No. 51401.
Engines: Two Leyland 680/1, 150 hp diesel engines per power car.
Transmission: Cardan shaft and freewheel to four-speed epicyclic gearbox, then cardan shaft to final drive on inner axle of each bogie.
Weight: Powered cars: 36.5 tons. Un-powered/trailer car: 30 tons.
Dimensions, each vehicle: 64' 0" x 9' 3" (19.5 x 2.82 m).
Connecting gangways: GWR suspension type, originally built as non-connecting-gangway units.
Bogies: Powered cars: DD10. Un-powered car: DT9.
Seating capacity: DMBS: 65 Second class.
TCL: 22 First Class + 48 Second Class + 2 Lavatories.
DMS: 89 Second Class.
Original owner: British Railways (WR).
Current owner: Nene Valley Railway.

These diesel-mechanical multiple units were originally built for British Railways Western Region as 3-car, non-connecting-gangway suburban units. They were displaced in the 1990s by the arrival of the Thames *Turbo* Class 165 DMUs.
The three cars that now make up the NVR set were originally allocated to the Thames Valley suburban services working out of London Paddington, although they were not then part of the same set. The following account briefly traces the story of each of these cars, leading to their eventual three-car formation on the Nene Valley Railway.

Driving Motor Brake Second (DMBS) No. 51347.

This powered car was delivered to Southall Depot in May 1960 with other cars 59499 and 51389, the three-car set eventually being re-allocated to Reading in March 1967. The set was repainted blue and took pride of place transporting thousands of enthusiasts to the Old Oak Common Open day on 15th July 1967. In February 1968 the unit was transferred to Lara (Plymouth) only to be back at Reading in April 1968. The unit entered Swindon Works in 1972 to be fitted with connecting gangways.

In 1983, during general refurbishment, the set was repainted into blue and grey. Under sectorisation in 1986 Reading came under Network South East and in February 1988 the set was painted in their house colours. On 12th July 1986, 51347 was used in the Fen Tiger Rail Tour which started from Reading, taking in Peterborough, Wisbech, Kings Lynn and Cambridge, as part of its itinary. It was transferred to Old Oak Common Depot on 28th September 1992, where its centre car (59499) was removed. The two remaining cars, 51347 and 51389 were then transferred to Tyseley and ran as a two-car unit until being withdrawn from service on

7th December 1993.

51347 was sold to Pressed Steel Heritage Ltd. in early 1994 and moved to Mangapps Railway Museum in April of that year. In April 1995 it moved to the Colne Valley Railway. During this time it was restored to green livery and eventually came to the Nene Valley Railway in April 1997.

Driving Motor Second (DMS) No. 51401.
This car was delivered to Southall Depot in July 1960 with cars 59511 and 51359. The 3-car set was reallocated to Reading in April 1967. It was repainted blue in the late 1960s and by 1971 was fitted with connecting gangways. Refurbished in the 1980s it was allocated to Network South East in 1986 and repainted in their house colours in 1987. The set was transferred to Old Oak Common in 1991 then back to Reading in 1992 when the set lost its centre car 59511. The now two-car set was re-allocated to Bletchley in 1993 to work services to Bedford on the North London Line. 51401 took part in a Branch Line Society Special to the Fenland area, in which the NVR was part of the itinerary, on the 19th February 1994. It was withdrawn by British Rail in October 1996, sold to Pressed Steel Heritage Ltd. and moved to the Nene Valley Railway in April 1997, to meet up with DMBS 51347. It was restored to green livery in 1998. So by this stage the NVR had a two-powered-car Diesel Multiple Unit (DMU) set.

Trailer Composite Lavatory (TCL) No. 59508.
This un-powered 'trailer' car was delivered to Southall depot in June 1960, to make up a three-car set with powered cars 51356 and 51398. The set (designated 1419) was re-allocated to Reading in 1967. During the late 1960s it was painted blue and fitted with gangways. In 1978 the set was sent to Swindon for refurbishment, gaining the short-lived white and blue livery. Under TOPS, centre cars were designated Class 176 until 1980 when they became Class 117, like the driving cars. 1986 saw the Network South East take over but it was not until early 1989 that their livery was applied to this set.

In 1992 Car No. 59508 left set 1419, joining set 836 with driving cars 51434 and 51503. After being withdrawn from service in 1993, 59508 entered preservation at the Battlefield Line, moving to the Nene Valley Railway on 24th September 1999, joining Cars 51347 and 51401, to make up the three car unit in service on the NVR today.

In 2000 Car 59508 was painted in the 1980s blue and grey livery to match 51347 and 51401, which had already been repainted.

The footsteps of all three DMU vehicles have been extended to allow for the additional platform side clearance arising from NVR's adoption of the European 'Berne' Gauge. (See description on pages 117 - 121).

During 2004 the three-car unit was temporarily taken out of service for the removal and replacement of its halon fire protection system, which had then become illegal due to its alleged toxicity risk.

From NVR's point of view, the greatest challenge from this three-car unit is that mechanically there are four of everything to keep an eye on - four engines, four gearboxes (which change gear simultaneously under the driver's control) and four drive-line systems. To keep all four engines and gearboxes running there is four times the need for re-usable spares. On the other hand, from the fitters' point of view, automotive rather than steam locomotive skills are the order of the day.

In late 2005 car DMBS 51347 had one of its engines replaced with a serviceable 'spare', in NVR's workshops. In early 2006 car DMS 51401 had a gearbox replacement and both power cars have had final drive replacements within the 2005-6 period. This four-engined, 224 seater train, now a 'heritage' unit in its own right, was of course the forerunner of the modern multiple unit train, offering greater operational flexibility in that it does not require locomotive run-round facilities at the end of the line and can, if necessary, run with one or more of its engines out of use. The set sees regular service on the Nene Valley Railway, especially in the quieter winter months when the push-button diesel engine starting is seen to greater advantage and of course on special Diesel Days.

DMU No. 59508 Trailer Composite Lavatory (Unpowered) at Wansford.

All photos: Brian Hallett

DMU No. 51347 Driving Motor Brake Second outside Wansford Workshops.

DMU No. 51401 Driving Motor Second at Wansford.

Continental Passenger Coaching Stock

French Nord Chemin de Fer Coach   No. B9Yf7122

This coach is a Second Corridor, with nine compartments and a toilet.

Coach No. 7122, of Type B9Yf, can seat 72 passengers and was built at Marly by Cie Industrielle de Material de Transport Ateliers du Rhonelle, for the Nord Chemin de Fer (North Railway of France) in 1928.

It was used on express traffic between Paris Nord and the northern ports of Calais and Boulogne until 1938, when the French Railways were nationalised. Surviving the Second World War, the coach was then most probably eventually used on semi-fast services all over the SNCF, as new rolling stock took over the faster services.

In 1983 the coach was purchased from SNCF by the British Science Museum as a companion to their Nord locomotive No. 3.628 and as an example of 'monocoque' stressed skin coach construction. The coach weighs 49.5 tonnes and is 22.35 metres long over the buffers. It was restored to the original Nord livery soon after delivery in 1983 and is owned by Chris Randall.

French 'Nord' coach No. B9Yf 7122 - note the very individual design of these coaches.   Photo: Brian Hallett

Norwegian State Railways (NSB) No. 601

This teak-bodied balcony-ended coach weighing 28 tons was built in 1922 for the Oslo suburban services, by Skabo Jernbanevogen Frabrick, Skoien Pr Kristania (Oslo after 1925) and served on these unspectacular duties until 1976.

Upon withdrawal from service by the Norwegian State Railways (NSB), No. 601 was purchased by Richard Hurlock and arrived on the Nene Valley Railway in January 1977.

No. 601 seats 76 passengers on reversible seats of the type once familiar on tram cars in Britain. On arrival on NVR No. 601 was fitted with electric heating and was thus used mainly in summer months as a strengthening vehicle on peak traffic days. However, it has since been equipped with steam heating by the NVR Carriage & Wagon Department, thus allowing it to be used in the winter months.

The gates on the centres of the balconies used to give access to adjoining vehicles fitted with continental type corridor connections, but for reasons of safety only NVR train staff may use these connections or ride on the balconies whilst the train is moving.

No. 601 featured in the James Bond film 'Octopussy' in which it was used as Octopussy's private car in the circus train.

When Richard Hurlock moved to the USA this vehicle was purchased by John Snasdell before being gifted to the Nene Valley Railway.

Norwegian Teak bodied coach No. 601 under the A1 bridge at Wansford.
Photo: Brian Hallett

Danish Passenger Coaching Stock

The Nene Valley Railway's six Danish coaches form the basis of the Continental train rake. They represent a design common throughout Europe.

The AUL was built in 1939 while the CL, CLS and CLE were built in the 1960s to a 1940 design for Copenhaven suburban or the Lille Nord, Slangenipbanen and Frederikssandbannen routes.

The CLS type were built with Berliner bogies from earlier teak CP type coaches, working the West Zone after being replaced by DMUs around Copenhagen, eventually being withdrawn from the late 1970s, some being sold to private railways in Denmark.

Scandia, Randers, built all the coaches for the Danish State Railways (DSB), fitted with air brakes and steam heating. Four arrived on the Nene Valley Railway in 1978, with a further two in 1983. Originally painted in DSB maroon they have since been painted in a wartime green.

Subsequently the coaches were allocated Nene Valley Railway numbers, but some have been re-numbered to their original DSB classification. UIC numbers were allocated in 1967.

All of these vehicles are owned by the NVR. Michael Fitton originally owned No. 261 but following his untimely death in 1981 his family donated the coach to the NVR.

Works No.	Veh. No.	NVR No.	Type	UIC No.	Built
24475	1674	475	CLE	50 86 8225674	1963
not available	261	476	AUL	50 86 3861261	1939
23913	1477	477	CL	50 86 2926477	1962 (1)
23914	1478	478	CL	50 86 2926478	1962
23219	1710	479	CLS	50 86 2927710	1961

Notes: (1) Scandia Bar. Eight seats removed to provide bar facilities. Now with 78 seats. Redesignated CLB. Carrying UIC No. 61 86 2926477.

Danish Coach Types:

CL: Later re-designated CLL in 1963/65.
Open with 86 Third Class seats, one toilet and a staff compartment.
Weight: 28.7 tons. 37 built in total.

AUL Re-designated AV in 1941, AVL in 1964 and ABh in 1969.
UIC re-numbered 50 86 3821261. Eight compartments which provide a total of 18 First and 40 Second Class seats. Two toilets.
Weight: 31 tons. 91 built in total.

CLE: Open Luggage Brake with 60 Third Class seats and one toilet.
Six seats have been removed to provide disabled accommodation. Now 54.
Weight 37 tons. 30 built in total.

CLS: 'Styne-Vogne' - Driving position for push-pull operation. Open, with 86 Third Class seats, one toilet and a staff compartment. Driving compartment is now used by NVR guards. Weight: 37 tons. 18 built in total.

Danish coach No. 475.

Danish coach No. 478.

Danish coach No. 476.

All photos: Brian Hallett

Danish coach No. 477.

Belgian Passenger Rolling Stock

There are four Belgian passenger coaches on the Nene Valley Railway, of three different types, each built in the 1930s at various Belgian works. Of the four coaches, three are of main line design, whilst the fourth is a suburban type.

The main line coaches are of high quality in terms of First Class travel, with different seat covers for smoking and non-smoking. These were used on main line traffic to and from Belgium's neighbouring countries - the Netherlands, Luxembourg and France.

The M1B type coaches were used on short distance commuter traffic or local country lines. All four Belgian coaches arrived at Wansford during 1990 and are owned by the Nene Valley Railway. Since arrival No. 21013 has been repainted in 'Wagon-Lits' First Class livery of blue and cream as has No. 21033 whilst the others remain in continental green.

First Class Coach Type K1A.
Nos. 21013 and 21033.
These coaches were built in 1934 by Baume et Marpent Ste Ame Haine-St-Pierre. They are First Class Open vehicles with two compartments and toilet. Each coach has 64 seats with six tip-up seats and weighs 43 tons.

Composite Coach Type K1AB.
No. 23009.
Built 1934 by La Brugeoise et Nicase & Dulcuve Societe Anonyme Division de Bruges. This is a First/Second Class coach with two compartments (1 First & 1 Second) and toilet, containing 28 First and 38 Second class seats in total (plus 6 tipup seats). Weight 43 tons.

Second Class Coach Type M1B.
No. 42170.
Built 1936 by Enghien et St. Elot.
This is a Second Class Open coach with 96 wooden seats and sliding doors. The coach weighs 45 tons.

Belgian Composite Coach Type K1AB No. 23009.

Belgian Built Wagon-Lits Sleeping Car No. 3916

'Voiture Lits' (or bed wagon) No. 3916 was built by Les Ateliers Metallurgiques de Nivelles, Belgium, in 1949, one of a series of 30 Class YT replacements for vehicles lost in the Second World War. Due to the urgency of the requirement, these vehicles were built to a pre-war design and were the last to incorporate the traditional Wagon-Lits inlaid wood panelling.

Because No. 3916 was to work the 'Nord Express', which ran from Paris and Ostend to Copenhagen, Stockholm and Oslo, it was built with two 3-berth compartments at each end and seven 2-berth compartments in the centre. The vehicle is multi-class: one berth First Class, two berths Second Class and three berths Third Class. After 1957, No. 3916 worked from Ostend to Germany, Austria and Switzerland. In 1960 it was transferred to Austria and added Italy to its itinerary. In 1964 it was moved to the Balkans and had regular turns from Munich to Athens and Ljubljana and particularly on the Brussels to Ljubljana car sleeper train. In 1975 No. 3916 joined the reserve fleet and was withdrawn on 31st December 1976.

No. 3916 was purchased in 1979 for use in a BBC television film which was made on the Nene Valley Railway and has since featured in several films. It is fully equipped and weighs 52 tons.

Car No. 3916 is ready for an external overhaul. It is parked in Wansford Yard.
Photo: Brian Hallett.

Italian Built Wagon-Lits Dining Car No. 2975

'Voiture Restaurant' No. 2975 was built by Officine Meccaniche Italiane at Reggio-Emilia, Italy, in 1927 one of a class of 75 vehicles which were the standard dining cars for use in ordinary express trains.

After initial service in Italy No. 2975 was allocated to Paris Nord and in 1931 to Vienna where its regular job was on the day trains to Basle. On the outbreak of war the vehicle was in Switzerland, where it remained in use on internal services until international running was resumed in 1949. It was then used on Basle to Milan services and during the 1950s it was regularly seen on the Scandinavia-Swiss-Italy Express between Frankfurt and Milan.

In 1963-4 No. 2975 was in Italy, working on trains between Milan and Domodossola. During this period the vehicle was fitted with a forced air extraction system with electric fans concealed behind a new ceiling. In 1965 No. 2975 was transferred to Amsterdam where it remained in use on holiday trains to Italy, the Cote D' Azure and the Spanish border, until withdrawn from service on 31st December 1977.

In 1978 the coach was purchased, in full working order, by Peterborough-based International travel specialists, Thomas Cook, who presented it on long-term loan to the Nene Valley Railway to mark the 50th Anniversary of Thomas Cook's association with Compagnie Internationale des Wagons-Lits et due Tourisme.

No. 2975 weighs 55.2 tonnes and seats 56 people. The fully equipped kitchen has an oil fired range and there is a coal fired heating and hot water boiler, which will heat the car if no steam is available from the locomotive.

No. 2975 was in regular use on NVR trains and is currently awaiting restoration. It is believed to be the heaviest passenger vehicle to have been in regular use anywhere in Britain.

Italian Built No. 2975 looking resplendent at Wansford.   Photo: B. Hallett.

Post Office Rolling Stock - Introduction

The Nene Valley Railway currently has four former BR Mark 1 Travelling Post Office (TPO) coaches that forms just part of the railway's TPO collection, which also includes three other TPOs from different periods - the largest collection of TPOs in preservation.

When BR started to build its fleet of passenger Mark 1's in the early 1950s it did not build any TPOs to the same basic design, instead continuing to build TPOs to an LMS design, similar to M30272M. By the late 1950s many of the TPOs in operation required replacing and the new Mark 1 TPOs started to appear from 1959, with the last one being built in 1977 - long after the last Mark 1 passenger vehicle had been built.

The first vehicles built in 1959 were of all new construction, but later batches reused passenger coaches that had become redundant.

The last TPOs were built in 1977 and replaced the final pre-nationalisation designed TPO coaches in service to give a total of 145 BR Mark 1 TPOs. These vehicles continued in service until the night of 9th/10th January 2004, when the final TPO services ran for the last time, although most of the vehicles built in 1959 were withdrawn in the 1990s.

The vehicles in our collection are:-

Number	Type	Year Built	Built At	Diagram	Lot Number	Initial Allocation.
80327	Sorter	1968/9	York	728	30778	Western Region.
80337	Sorter	1968/9	York	729	30779	Eastern Region.
80402	Stowage	1959	Wolverton	722	30488	Western Region.
80456	Brake Stowage	1968	York	733	30782	Midland Region.

Notes:

80327 was built with provision for traductor arms, but not for nets. On 20th June 1995 the carriage was named "George James" at Penzance station in recognition of over 40 years service to the TPOs by Penzance based George James. This vehicle was also the last but one TPO to be given a major overhaul.

80337 was built with the ability to carry exchange equipment, but never carried it in service. This vehicle was modified in later years to include a system called "Priority Service". The vehicle was in use on the final night of the TPO services when it formed part of the Great Western TPO.

80402 was built with both an apparatus net and traductor arms. The vehicle is the only mark1 stowage van with apparatus ability to survive, the other two, 80400 and 80401 both having been scrapped.

80456 was built with a brake compartment at one end to accommodate a guard. This enabled complete rakes of TPOs to be marshalled without the need to use any passenger carrying brake vehicles.

TPO Vehicle No. 80327 in Euston storage sidings awaiting despatch to NVR

TPO No. 80337 also awaits in Euston sidings.   Photo: Paul Ruston

Although not specifically built as a Post Office vehicle this coach is included in this section as its design has always made it suitable for 'parcels' traffic and it now 'belongs' to the NVR TPO Group.

This coach was built at Wolverhampton in 1938, Lot No. 1096 to Diagram 2007.

These vehicles were common throughout the LMS, being used in all types of trains, from expresses to milk trains. Some of the coaches remained in use as late as 1984, surviving as parcels vans, often without corridor connections. This particular vehicle, numbered M30976M, was being used as a stores van in 1976, allocated the Departmental No. DB 975562.

It was preserved in 1989 as the stores vehicle for the 5532 Group, being their first vehicle at Ruabon. From Ruabon it was moved to the Llangollen Railway for Signal & Telegraph Department use. It was sold to the Nene Valley Railway TPO Group on 21st April 1999, arriving at Wansford on 12th September 2000.

No. 30976 is intended for use with TPO M30272M and LMS rake of coaches.

LMS No. 30976 Passenger Brake Van. Photo: Brian Hallett.

No. 2178, six wheeled Great Northern Railway TPO coach, built in 1885.
Seen here on its temporary chassis at Wansford. Photo:
E. Craggs.
See page 97 for further details.

SR Travelling Post Office (TPO)   No. 4920

Built 1939, Eastleigh, Lot No. 1043 to Diagram 3192.

This vehicle was first used on the Southern Railway night postal service from Waterloo to Weymouth and Exeter, on the former South Western routes. It was then transferred to the Eastern Division for use on the Dover night postal service, until withdrawn in 1977.

It was claimed for the National Collection and, in 1977, was placed on loan to the Nene Valley Railway. The coach now stands in Platform 4, Wansford Station and houses the NVR Exhibition, which includes the original Post Office racking where visitors can try their hand at fast mail sorting. It is now owned by the NVR.

Southern Region Travelling Post Office Vehicle No. 4920.   Photo: B. Hallett.

GREAT NORTHERN TPO No. 2178 (Body)

GNR TPO 2178 was built by the Great Northern Railway at Doncaster in 1885 as a sorting vehicle with two traductor arms and a high sided net to perform exchanges using lineside apparatus. 2178 was the first of four vehicles built to diagram 319 and had a corridor connector at one end only, is 34 feet long and was originally built on a six wheel chassis.

2178 is listed as being withdrawn from service in March 1935, but it is known that it was delivered to the allotments at Balby, Doncaster during 1927, as a report including a picture appeared in a local paper of the time.

The NVR were made aware of its existence in late 2004 and the vehicle was duly inspected in early 2005. As the body was found to be in a very good condition the vehicle was acquired by the NVR's TPO group and collected by road on Friday 26th August 2005. On arrival at Wansford the body was unloaded onto a flat wagon. It is planned to fully restore the vehicle in the fullness of time, including the building of a replacement chassis to enable it to operate once again.

The body is all teak and has been preserved well by the allotment society, who built lean-tos on either side of the vehicle and then protected the whole vehicle and lean-tos with roofing felt. The allotment society also preserved some of the internal features by reusing many parts, for example the sliding doors for the corridor connector were taken out and used as shelving.

BR(M) LMSR Travelling Post Office (TPO)No. M30272M

Built 1949 at Wolverton. Lot 1559 to Diagram 2167.

This vehicle is fitted with lineside apparatus to pick up and drop off mail whilst on the move. In 1963 this vehicle was involved in an infamous incident which became known as the Great Train Robbery, although this information only recently became available. M30272M was the tenth vehicle in the twelve coach train and is the only one to survive in preservation.

It was preserved in 1974 for the National Collection and stored at Brighton until 1977, when it was moved to the National Railway Museum, York. Due to lack of space at York, 30272 was moved to Tyseley in 1984.

As a result of a Board of Survey by the NRM in 1996 the coach was donated to the Nene Valley Railway. It arrived at Wansford on the 9th August 1996 and is currently being restored to working order by the Friends of M30272M TPO Group.

The NVR has obtained the lineside apparatus, on loan from the Locomotive Club of Great Britain and the Sittingbourne and Kemsley Light Railway, for use with the vehicle when restoration is complete. In the meantime, however, NVR holds an annual Rail Mail Weekend in June when the lineside apparatus can be seen working with a visiting TPO vehicle from the Didcot Railway Centre or the Great Central Railway.

The first lineside apparatus is sited at 'Sutton Cross' which is around a mile east of Wansford station. A second apparatus is soon to be installed approaching the new Yarwell Halt. This operation is well worth seeing!

An exterior view showing progress on M30272M in June 2006. The vehicle is almost ready for its external panelling.

Both Photos: Brian Hallett.

Showing the interior progress on M30272M. In this June 2006 view most of the interior is in place.

NVR Freight Rolling Stock - Introduction

Over the years the Nene Valley Railway has acquired a wide selection of well over 60 freight vehicles, ranging in age and size from a 1910 LNWR Gunpowder van, a 3-plank wooden sided LMS open wagon built in 1935, to a 1961, 40 ton 'Flatrol' wagon last used on the East Coast Main Line Electrification. There are many traditional 4-wheeled vehicles, of course, a small selection of 6-wheelers and a variety of bogie vehicles. There is currently one Continental freight vehicle, from Denmark.

The NVR collection of freight vehicles holds a wide attraction for the freight railway enthusiast as well as for freight railway modellers, concentrating their attention on the minutest constructional details.

The freight vehicles are mostly owned by NVR members or by the groups that are located on the Railway. It is hoped the collection will continue to grow as availability of vehicles, space and finances allow.

The freight vehicles are grouped on the following pages under the following general headings:- Pre-nationalisation Railway Companies, Private Owner Vehicles, British Rail Open Wagons, Vanfits, Other BR vans and a Continental Vehicle.

Many of the freight vehicles are in full running order and are periodically run in demonstration freight trains, hauled by a variety of locomotives, on special-event days. When not in use they can be seen standing in sidings at Wansford, Ferry Meadows and at Peterborough Nene Valley Station adjacent to the Railworld Centre, where a further 3 freight vehicles are on separate display.

Some NVR freight vehicles are no longer in running order, but are retained because of their interest or heritage value.

There is always a need for more volunteers to assist in the maintenance of the running freight vehicles and to restore others to running order or to 'display' condition.

BR 22T Plate Wagon No. B931807

31 T Tank No. BPO 64172

British Pre-Nationalisation Freight Rolling Stock LMS Group Vehicles

LNWR Gunpowder Van No. 11023.
Built 1910, Wolverton.
Ex Peterborough Sugar Factory.

LNWR 6-Wheeled Covered Combination Truck (CCC) No. DM395361.
Built circa 1920, Wolverton to Diagram 444a.
It was last used by BR in departmental use for weighing machine maintenance.

LNWR 8-plank Open Wagon No. P143288.
Built 1919, probably at Wolverton, with wooden frames.
Last used at Peterborough Sugar Factory.
Now restored as 'Peterborough Coal & Coke.'

LNWR 7-plank Open Wagon No. P208445.
Built 1920, probably at Wolverton, with wooden frames.
Acquired from Peterborough Sugar Factory.

MR 5-plank Open Wagon No. 3285.
Probably built at Derby, with wooden frames.
It also carried the number 92356 and was acquired from Baker Perkins Ltd., Peterborough.

LMS 3-plank Open Wagon No. 470944.
Built 1935 by Hurst Nelson, Motherwell.
Last used by BR Electrification Department, Peterborough.

LMS CCT Vans Nos. 37066, 37071, 37096 and 37141.
Built 1938 by Metro-Cammell, Saltley, Birmingham. Lot No. 1154 to diagram 2026.

LMS 20 ton Hopper Wagon No. 691535.
Built 1938 by Metro-Cammell, Saltley, Birmingham.
Used on iron ore traffic during its BR career.
Acquired from Peterborough Sugar Factory as No. 15.

LMS 14 ton ESSO Oil Tank Wagon No. 1914.
(LMS Registered No. 162368)
Built 1941 by Hurst Nelson, Motherwell.

LMS 13 ton 7-plank Open Wagon No. 237950.
Built 1942. Wooden frames.
Last used by British Leyland, Wellingborough. Now restored as 'CWS Ltd' No. 2379.

A SELECTION OF FREIGHT VEHICLES ON THE NVR

No. 237950

LNWR 395361

No. 470944

No. 691535

No. 764034

No. 427960

No. DB 972594.
Photo:
Robert Maskill.

All photographs by Brian Hallett with the exception of DB972594.

British Pre-Nationalisation Freight Rolling Stock
LNER Group Vehicles

GREAT NORTHERN RAILWAY (GNR) VEHICLES:

'Lowmac' Flat Wagon No. 414030.
Built 1909, Doncaster. No further information currently available.

Lowmac No. 414030

LONDON & NORTH EASTERN RAILWAY (LNER) VEHICLES:

Plywood Body Van No. 298132. (Grounded Body).
Built 1946. Other details of origin unknown.
Located at Peterborough Nene Valley Station.

Hopper Wagon Chassis No. 7.
Built 1937 by Hurst Nelson, Motherwell.
Used as a water tank base, Peterborough Sugar Factory (No. 7).
Now used as a flat wagon.

British Freight Rolling Stock: Other Regional Groups and Private Owner Freight Vehicles.

SOUTHERN REGION (SR) VEHICLES:

25 ton Brake Van No. 55550.
Built 1928, probably Ashford. Lot No. 1578.

12 ton 5-plank Open Wagon No. 5869.
Date and builder unknown.

GROUNDED VAN At Peterborough Nene Valley Station.
12 ton Ventilated Van Body No. B760049.

GROUNDED VANS At Wansford Station:
12 ton Ventilated Van Bodies Nos. B755864, B762042 and B785705.

12 ton SHOCVAN Bodies Nos. B851452 and B851860.

12 ton Ventilated Fruit Van Body No. 875739.

Internal User No. 041336

PRIVATE OWNER FREIGHT VEHICLES:

KETTON CEMENT 4-plank Open Tippler No. 9.
Built circa 1929 at Ketton Cement Works using parts purchased from older wagons.
No. 9 has LNWR stamped on certain components.

SHELL-MEX 32 ton Tank Wagon No. 5181.
Built 1965 by Metro-Cammell, Saltley.
Later TOPS No. BPO 64172.
BR Registered No. 185927.

British Nationalised Freight Rolling Stock
British Railways Open Wagons.

13 ton High Goods Wagon 'Hi-Shock' No. B721890.
Built 1952, Derby. Lot No. 2317 to Diagram 1/040. Fitted with sheet support rail.

17 ton Fitted Ballast Hopper Wagon 'Mackerel', No. B992358.
Built 1951 by Metro-Cammell, Saltley, Birmingham. Lot No. 2264.

22 ton Low Dropside Open Wagon 'Plate', No. B931807.
Built 1953, Shildon. Lot No. 2476.

21 ton Mineral Hopper Wagons:
No. B425561.
Built 1957 by Head Wrightson. Lot No. 3033 to Diagram 1/146.

No. B427960.
Built 1957 by Charles Roberts. Lot No. 3037 to Diagram 1/146.

No. B430226.
Built 1958, Shildon. Lot No. 3120 to Diagram 1/149.

No. B431752.
Built 1958 by Pressed Steel. Lot No. 3157 to Diagram 1/146.

25 ton Ballast Hopper Wagon 'Trout', No. B992164.
Built 1951 by Metro-Cammell, Saltley, Birmingham. Lot No. 2188.

25 ton 'Lowmac' Wagon No. B904523.
Built 1950 by P & W McLellan Ltd. Lot No. 2187 to Diagram 2/248.

30 ton Hot Pig-Iron Wagon No. B744647.
Built 1956, Shildon. Lot No. 2857 to Diagram 1/005.

30 ton Bogie Bolster 'C' Wagon No. B945991.
Original number and date of rebuild unknown but believed to be to Diagram 1/477.
Acquired from Mobil Oil Co., Thameshaven, Coryton.

31 ton Plate Wagon No. 460411.
Built 1979, Shildon. Lot No. 3839 to Design Code SP020A. Last used by Balfour Beatty for possession work only and given an Internal No. XTZ7637 by its owners who used it to carry a generator for track 'vacuum cleaner'. Later donated to NVR.

40 ton Bogie 'Flatrol' Wagon No. B901021.
Built 1961, Swindon. Lot No. 3194 to Diagram 2/748. Last used by BR Elec. Dept.

32 ton Steel Carrying Wagon No. DC400053
Built 1970, Ashford. Lot No. 3728 to Design Code SA001A?B.

British Nationalised Freight Rolling Stock
British Railways 'Vanfits'

With the dawn of nationalisation of British Railways, standard rolling stock designs were developed to replace the stock damaged or destroyed in the Second World War. The standard 12 ton ventilated van design came about as a result of the amalgamation of the 'Big Four' railway companies. There were three 'Diagrams' relating to the vehicles construction:-

Diagram 1/208   Tongued and grooved planked sides and doors, although some were given plywood doors. A total of 19,063 such vans were built, in 22 different lots.

Diagram 1/213   Plywood sides and doors. a total of 3,699 were built.

Diagram 1/224   Plywood sides and doors, with Oleo buffers fitted. A total of 1,000 such vans were built in 1961 by Pressed Steel Ltd., under Lot No. 3398.

In the summer of 1992, 20 Vanfits were discovered at the British Sugar Corporation Factory at Spalding, South Lincolnshire. The BSC had purchased them from British Rail in the early 1980s for conversion to canvas sides for transporting pallets around the factory complex. The 'prototype' was unsuccessful, however, so the 20 Vanfits became storage vehicles.

An agreement was reached for the vans to be moved to the Nene Valley Railway and the first one (B771300) arrived at Wansford on 1st August 1992. That same week a film company enquired if the Railway had 15 or so identical wagons. They were told that there *were* vans owned by NVR but that they were at Spalding. Since they were needed urgently the film company agreed to move them with all haste to Wansford. The last three arrived at Wansford on 8th August 1992, just seven days later! The full story can be read in *Nene Steam* No.41.

As the future of freight traffic depended on speed, a large number of these vans were fitted with vacuum brakes. All those now preserved on the Nene Valley Railway were so fitted, but the vacuum cylinders were removed by BR. It is hoped to completely refit some of the vans in the future.

Ventilated Van styles Centre: No.761651

Nene Valley Railway 12 ton Vanfits:

BR Number	BSC No.	Builder	Year Built	Lot No.	Diagram
B759852	61*	Wolverton	1952	2310	1/208
B761651	69*	Wolverton	1952	2465	1/208
B764034	66	Wolverton	1953	2541	1/208
B768248	63*	Wolverton	1955	2707	1/208
B771300	54	Wolverton	1956	2841	1/208
B774874	60*	Wolverton	1957	2991	1/208
B775176	67*	Wolverton	1957	2991	1/208
B775702	59	Faverdale	1957	3007	1/213
B776607	53*	Ashford	1957	3023	1/213
B777633	65	Wolverton	1958	3086	1/208
B777654	52	Wolverton	1958	3086	1/208
B778019	56	Wolverton	1958	3086	1/208
B780952	68*	Charles Roberts	1958	3164	1/208
B781387	62*	Charles Roberts	1958	3164	1/208
B781542	51*	Charles Roberts	1958	3164	1/208
B785122	70	Pressed Steel	1961	3398	1/224
B785409	64*	Pressed Steel	1961	3398	1/224
B785619	55	Pressed Steel	1961	3398	1/224
B786075	57*	Pressed Steel	1961	3398	1/224

BR Internal User

B785522 (BR) 024461		Pressed Steel	1961	3398	1/224

Last used at
Wolverhampton

* **Restored, therefore BSC number no longer exists (at the time of writing).**

Vanfit No. B786075
Body sides made of ply.
Weather proof resin-bonded
plywood was used.

Vanfit No. B771300.
Note the tongued and grooved timber
boarded body-side construction.

British Nationalised Freight Rolling Stock
British Railways Vans - (excluding Vanfits)

12 ton Pallet Van 'Palvan' No. B781768.
Built 1960 at Wolverton. Lot No. 3310 to Diagram 1/211.

12 ton Pallet Van 'Palvan' No. B778810.
Built 1958, Faverdale. Lot No. 3191 to Diagram 1/211
Also carried Internal User No. 041108.

12 ton Banana Van No. B881987.
Built 1959 at Wolverton. Lot No. 3029 to Diagram 1.

Fish Van SPV (Special Purpose Van) No. 75169.
Built 1948, Faverdale to Diagram 214. Used on fish trains until used by Doncaster works for transferring spares to March and Cambridge. Later transferred to the Internal Fleet at Doncaster Works and renumbered 041255.

Parcel Van (CCT) No. 94796.
Built 1961, Earlstown. Lot No. 30614 to diagram 816.

20 ton Brake Van No. B953944.
Chassis, Flat Wagon 'Queen Mary'. Built 1958, Faverdale. Lot No. 3129.

20 ton Brake Van No. 954024.
Built 1959, Faverdale. Lot No. 3129. Later used by British Steel Corporation, Scunthorpe, with No. BSC 7606.
Preserved at the Rutland Railway Museum before being moved to the NVR.

Continental Freight Rolling Stock
Danish State Railways (DSB)

Bogie Flat Wagon No. 8959.
Built 1927 by Scania, Randers.
Original dropside wagon with hinged sides so that it could carry ballast.
These have been removed since arrival on the Nene Valley Railway, as it has always been used as a flat wagon.
In 1989 a film crew transformed the vehicle into a stage on rails for the pop group 'Queen's' video 'Breakthrough'. After the filming the underframe was given attention and painted. It was at this time the number 8959 was discovered.

PLATELAYER'S VEHICLES

This is the 'Luxury' model.
The Wickham petrol driven railcar
Great Eastern Railway platelayer's No. 01044. Built in 1944 and based at pump trolley. Built 1907. Man powered. Oundle.

Engineering/Permanent Way Vehicles - Introduction

The Nene Valley Railway Civil Engineering Department has its own fleet of rail vehicles. These range from flat wagons and ballast hoppers to the TASC 45 track machine. These vehicles see regular use by the 'Civils', in and out of season, for maintenance and renewal work on NVR's tracks, bridges and other parts of the railway's infrastructure.

There is also the 40 ton steam crane which 'belongs' to the mechanical Engineering Department but its services are frequently needed by the Civils for permanent way work.

The principle difference between these engineering/permanent way vehicles and NVR's other freight rolling stock is that the former see regular use in keeping NVR's tracks up to standard - so that passenger and 'heritage' freight trains can keep 'rolling'.

So, on the engineering side - indeed as throughout the entire railway - there is a backbone of mutual dependency and a continual need for cross-department co-operation.

The steam crane at rest in Wansford yard.
Photo: David Withers.

Engineering Rail Vehicles
LMS 40 ton Steam Crane

Country of origin: United Kingdom
Builders: Ransomes & Rapier Ltd., Ipswich. (Works No. D2958). Year: 1930.
Number of cylinders: 2 (for hoist and slew only). Boiler pressure: 120 psi.
Locomotive traction required.
Weight: 108 tons. Maximum lift: 40 tons.
Original owner: London, Midland & Scottish Railway Company. (LMS)
Current owner: Nene Valley Railway.

This LMS 40 ton capacity steam breakdown crane No. MP3 was built by Ransomes & Rapier Ltd., Ipswich, in 1930, to Order No. D2958. Originally built as a 36 ton capacity machine, MP3 was allocated to Kentish Town Depot, London, which served the southern end of the LMS line to St Pancras.

The machine is carried on 4 axles with weight-relieving 2-axle bogies fore and aft. The crane runner vehicle, which carries the jib when stowed for travelling, is No. ADM 299850, built at Derby in 1931.

In 1939 MP3 was uprated to 40 tons lift capacity and moved to Holbeck Depot, Leeds. In 1941 it was renumbered RS1004 under the LMS crane renumbering scheme.

In 1954 the then British Railways transferred Holbeck Depot and its rolling stock allocation to the North Eastern Region and the new management renumbered this crane to No. 159. Under a subsequent reorganisation the North Eastern Region was abolished and the Leeds area was taken over by the Eastern Region, who renumbered No. 159 yet again, to ADE331159.

In the early 1970s the BR TOPS System was introduced. Steam cranes were included and ADE331159 was allocated the TOPS identification number ADRV95207.

As steam cranes were progressively phased out by the introduction of diesel machines during the 1970s, ADE331159 was moved to Doncaster, where it acted as standby unit until withdrawn, being the last remaining steam breakdown crane on the Eastern Region. ADE331159 is vacuum piped for travelling to operating sites at speeds of up to 45 mph.

The crane was purchased by the Nene Valley Railway in December 1982 and renovation work has continued progressively, subject to availability of time and personnel in between the more immediate demands of NVR service locomotives. The most substantial and challenging item to receive attention in Wansford Workshops was the crane's boiler, which was not the original 1930s unit, but a larger one fitted in BR days. This boiler was removed from the crane, to be re-barrelled by outside specialists and received its ten-year certificate in 2002. Refitting it to the crane necessitated modification work on the roof and other parts of the cab, to remove the 'hammer and torch' appearance and other 'quick fixes' left by the earlier BR boiler change, thus restoring the machine as far as possible to its original 1930s appearance. Other restoration work has included substantial re-riveting of parts of the cab and match wagon, new timber flooring of the latter, attention to the hoist and swing machinery, the ropes and pulleys and cleaning up and repainting of the complete machine in bright red with the jib head in white, as it was when stationed at Leeds Holbeck in BR days.

The jib was raised under the crane's own steam for the first time in over two years on 12th February 2003. One of the refurbished crane's first duties was in Wansford Yard, lifting *City of Peterborough's* boiler, during the locomotive's rebuild.

Of all-riveted construction, the crane is a fascinating example of early 20th Century heavy railway crane design. Its two steam cylinders drive a cross-shaft on which are situated the reversing gear selector clutches and the gears for operating the main hoist, jib hoist and slewing. All this machinery is of 'open' design and most of it can be seen from ground level.

The crane is currently used whenever heavy lifts are required by NVR's Mechanical Engineering Department, typically locomotive boiler handling and by the Civil Engineers for handling track work etc.

The steam crane at work in Wansford Yard.
Photo: Roy Harrison.

40 ton Track and Service Car (TASC)   Photo: Roy Harrison.

Engineering & Permanent Way Rail Vehicles
40 ton Track and Service Car (TASC) No. 98500

Country of origin: UK.
Builder: Plasser (GB) Ltd.   Year 1985.   Works Number 52788.
Engine: Deutz V-8, air-cooled diesel.
Transmission: ZF 3-speed, fully reversing, power shift gearbox.
Mounted on four wheels but driven on two only, at the truck body/hoist end.
Wheels diameter: 28".   Maximum self-propelled speed: 40 mph.   Brakes: Air.
Machine weight: 20 tons, excluding later modifications (see below).
Auxiliary Deutz diesel engine and generator provide power for electrical services.
Original owner: British Rail, then Amey Rail Fleet Services Ltd.
Current owner: Nene Valley Railway.

The name Plasser and Theurer has become synonymous with rail renewal and maintenance machinery and there are over 200 Plasser machines in service on Britain's railways.

This machine, No. 98500 was the first of a short series of seven such machines built in the UK for use on minor permanent way and trackside work. Fitted with RETB and radio telephone, the machine is ideally suited for working at more remote work sites and was believed to have been used for track inspection and minor works on Scotland's West Highland Line.

The combined mess room/driver's cab has dual controls for driving in each direction, but the transmission can be isolated and the machine towed in a train. Mess room facilities include a 'Belling' cooker, stainless steel sink and table and chairs seating accommodation for about eight on-board personnel. A services control panel mounted on the side of the machine and accessed from the trackside, includes a 'Tea Boiler' switch!

The machine is fitted with lights for night/tunnel working and electrical power take-off points for the use of portable tools.

The truck body measures 14' 4" x 8' 3" x 20" (7.3 cubic yard capacity), has drop sides and can be hydraulically tipped either side. A tail-end mounted Atlas 2.2 ton hydraulic lift arm (a larger one than that which was originally installed) with stabilisers can be fitted with a lift hook or a grab for handling loose material. This lift arm can work over its own truck body or over an attached open wagon. No. 98500 was also later modified with the fitting of hydraulic buffers and air braking equipment for an attached wagon.

The machine was taken out of service on BR in mid 1998 due to its alleged non-reliability at that time to operate track circuits, being only a two-axle vehicle. No. 98500 was stored for some years at Perth Depot, where it was subject to vandalism and the 'borrowing' of parts for sister machines. It was donated to the Nene Valley Railway by Amey Rail Fleet Services Ltd. in February 2005.

A programme of restoration is now under way by NVR Mechanical and Civil Engineering Group members, as time permits alongside their other work. Replacements for missing parts are being sought. New side windows have already been fitted, courtesy Plasser Machinery Parts and Service Ltd., who have already been most helpful to NVR sourcing information, parts, etc. All-in-all, this is an ideal machine for the NVR 'behind-the-scenes and out-of-season' teams and alongside an

ever growing list of 'jobs', the machines return to working condition is eagerly await-
ed by the Civil Engineering and Signal & Telegraph (S & T) Departments.

'Sealion' 40 ton Ballast Hoppers Numbers DB 982721 and 982725.
These two wagons are dual (air and vacuum) braked and have both side and centre
discharge. the discharge being operated from each end of the vehicle.
They were both purchased from EWS at Peterborough Eastfield Yard and arrived at
the Nene Valley Railway on 8th April 2005.
No. DB982721 was first used on NVR track ballasting on 13th April 2005.

'Rudd' Engineers' Open Wagons Numbers DB 972206, 972594 and 984194.
These 21 ton capacity, air braked wagons were introduced in 1989 and consist of new
bodies built onto under-frames from redundant hopper wagons. Rudd wagons are
basically designed for engineers' use, their low drop sides and substantial steel floors
suiting them to on-site loading and unloading of spent ballast, spoil, sleepers, etc.

No. DB972594 arrived on NVR on 18th April 2005, the two other wagons
following at later dates. No. DB984194 was converted from a 'Grampus' to a 'Rudd'
wagon, so has a slightly different construction to the other two.

At the time of writing (Spring 2006) all three NVR 'Rudds' have been in use
for spoil removal in preparation for track realignment at the site of the new Yarwell
Junction station and at Wansford Yard on site preparation for the new locomotive
workshop.

14 ton 'Lowmac' Wagon Number B905053.
Built 1953 at Shildon. Lot No. 2475 to Diagram 2/244.
Last used by BR Electrification Department, who had fitted a Poclain TY-45
Hydraulic Excavator to dig out mast footings. Finally used at Peterborough before
withdrawal. The Poclain excavator has since been removed and scrapped by NVR,
rendering the wagon suitable for transporting engineering materials and equipment.

'Shark' Brake Van/Ballast Plough Number DB993836.
Built 1957 by British Railways Carriage and Wagon Company.
Owner: Steve King.
Although at first appearance a conventional brake van, technically the 'Shark' is a
civil engineer's tool so is included here.

This vehicle is one of 226 combined brake van and ballast ploughs built for
British Railways between 1952 and 1962. It spent its entire working life in the north-
east of England, based at Tyne Yard, Gateshead.

Originating from an LMS design the 'Shark' features two steel 'ploughs'
(presumably so named because of the similarity in appearance with a snow plough
rather than an agricultural implement) or levelling blades, mounted one at each end,
one for each direction of working. When working with a loose coupled ballast train
the 'Shark' acts as a conventional brake van, providing braking assistance for the
train as required. However, when the train is laying ballast between the running
rails the 'Sharks' plough spreads and levels the ballast across the full width of the
sleepers, ready for the next operation.

With the demise of loose-coupled ballast hoppers, these vehicles now being
vacuum or air braked, brake vans became redundant, but 'Sharks' can still be seen in
their main role levelling ballast on Britain's railways.

It has been suggested that these vehicles are probably the oldest in main line service today. About a dozen 'Sharks' are believed to be in preservation.

The short (9 ft) wheel base, necessitated by the blades being mounted *outside* the wheel base, results in rough riding and the 'Sharks' are restricted to 45 mph on main line work.

No. DB993836 was acquired by the present owner from EWS, Leicester. The vehicle is being progressively restored by its owner. A 'hot box' fault has already been rectified and work is proceeding on the cabin 'body work'. It is anticipated that the 'Shark' will be used by NVR Civil Engineers for ballast spreading when required.

The following 'vehicles', although included here with functioning NVR Engineering/Permanent Way equipment are not in working order but are preserved on the NVR as heritage machines (See pictures on page 108):-

Wickham Permanent Way Railcar Number 01044.
Petrol driven.   Built 1944.   Formerly based at Oundle.

Great Eastern Railway Platelayers' (PW) Pump Trolley.
Built 1907. subsequently rebuilt.

SharkBrake Van/Ballast Plough No. DB993836

Photo: E. Craggs.

40T Sea Lions Nos. DB982725 and DB982721   Photo: R. Maskill.

Appendix A: Metrication

In keeping with the spirit of the Heritage Railways movement, the original 'Imperial' units of measure for all UK and USA-originated locomotives and rolling stock are quoted throughout this book. Imperial units are also quoted for most of the Continental locomotives and rolling stock, this data having been converted from the original Metric figures.

However, ISO-Metric units have been taught in UK schools and colleges now for well over 30 years. Furthermore, since some UK pre-metrication abbreviations (e.g:- psi, mph), although in common use and well understood by all concerned, even then did not comply with the British Standards abbreviations of the day, it is to be expected that much of the numerical data contained in these pages may appear obscure to NVR's younger generation visitors, as well as to the ever-increasing numbers of our visitors from overseas.

Keeping academic explanations to an absolute minimum, the guidance notes below are provided for a quick-and-easy reference for all who wish to make a comparison between the old and the new. They should not be used for any other purpose.

A pocket electronic calculator (or an arithmetic brain) will come in handy!

LENGTH
Multiply inches by **25.4** to obtain millimetres (mm).
Multiply feet by **0.305** to obtain metres (m).
Multiple miles by **1.609** to obtain Kilometres (Km).
Note that centimetres (cm) are NOT in common use in engineering.

AREA
Multiply square inches by **645** to obtain square millimetres (mm^2).
Multiply square feet by **0.0929** to obtain square metres (m^2).

VOLUME OR CAPACITY
Multiply gallons by **4.546** to obtain litres (1).
Multiply cubic feet by **28.32** to obtain litres (1).

WEIGHT
Multiply pounds (lb) by **0.4536** to obtain Kilogrammes (Kg).
Multiply tons by **1.016** to obtain tonnes.

FORCE (as in a locomotive's tractive effort)
Multiply pounds (lbf) by **0.00448** to obtain Kilonewtons (KN).

PRESSURE
Multiply pounds per square inch (psi) by **0.6895** to obtain bar.

SPEED
Multiply miles per hour (mph) by **1.609** to obtain Kilometres per hour (Km/h).

POWER
Multiply horsepower (hp) by **0.746** to give Kilowatts (KW).

EXAMPLES
Converted in this way the relevant data for **Class B1 Locomotive** *Mayflower* becomes:
Number of cylinders: **(508mm x 660mm)**. Boiler Pressure: **155.1375 bar.**
Driving Wheels diameter: **1,880mm.**   Weight: **125.628 tonnes** or 125,628 Kg.
For **Class 40 Diesel Locomotive D306** *Atlantic Conveyor* the relevant data becomes:
Engine: English Electric 16SVT Mk11 **(1,492 KW** @ 850 rev/min).
Tractive Effort: **233.9 KN.**   Driving Wheels diameter: **1,143 mm**

Maximum Speed: **145 Km/h.**

Take care if using the conversion factors shown on the previous page on data for Continental locomotives and rolling stock as the 'rounding up' or down may not give a return to the exact original Metric figures.

THE STANDARD RAIL TRACK GAUGE OF 4' 8^1/$_2$ " = 1,436 mm.

Appendix B: Steam Locomotive
Boiler Certificates and Overhaul

The following provides a brief background to the 'Ten Year Boiler Certificate' referred to in this book in connection with steam locomotives. This information is included in the Stock Book for the benefit of NVR visitors and others having a general interest in steam locomotives and should not be used for any other purpose.

Steam locomotive boilers, being pressure vessels and subject to extremes of temperature, pressure, corrosion and erosion are subject under the Law to various regulations including The Pressure Vessels Safety Regulations 2000.

In practical terms this requires that every steam locomotive boiler (this also includes steam cranes and other steam-powered machinery) used on a heritage railway must be inspected, hydraulically tested and certified by a suitably qualified person (usually, but not necessarily, acting on behalf of the company who will be insuring the locomotive) at the most, every TEN years. However annual inspections are also required.

On the expiry of the ten year period a thorough internal and external inspection of the boiler becomes mandatory. This virtually always necessitates the boiler being removed from the locomotive. The boiler is then inspected to establish its condition and the work required to give it a further working life, bearing in mind that the boiler must be pressure tight. X-ray, ultra-sonic and other modern inspection techniques are frequently used for this inspection work.

Once the renewal work has been done and this can be both extensive and expensive, as it is normally carried out by boiler specialists, the boiler is re-inspected, given a 'hydraulic' test with water pressure, then finally a steam pressure test.

In the meantime, with the boiler removed from the frames, attention can be given to inspecting, repairing and rebuilding the other parts of the locomotive, cylinders and pistons, valve gear, wheels and so on. You only have to look at the parts of a dismantled steam locomotive to appreciate the rugged complexity of the allegedly 'simple' steam locomotive.

Once the boiler has passed its mandatory tests its new Ten Year Certificate is issued and the ten year clock is ticking.

The boiler now has to be refitted to the locomotive, pipe work and controls fitted, the locomotive's external 'bodywork' put in place and the loco given its new livery before it can be put back into service. All this takes time on a heritage railway with a few full time fitters who also have to look after the railway's running locomotives and other rolling stock, supported by volunteers. This time is lost from the boiler's ten year certificate, so careful pre-planning is needed to minimise this lost time and to get the locomotive back to work as soon as possible.

The brief account (pages 11 & 12 in this book) of the recent re-build of No. 73050 *City of Peterborough* bears witness to the work carried out by the Nene Valley Railway workshop staff, in this respect.

Appendix C:
The 'Berne Gauge' and the Nene Valley Railway

The Nene Valley Railway is believed to be unique amongst UK Heritage Railways in that it conforms to the so called 'Berne' Load Gauge and can therefore accommodate Berne compliant Continental locomotives and rolling stock that are too large to operate on other UK railways.

To be strictly correct, there is no such thing *officially* as the 'Berne' Gauge but the information on these pages is provided in good faith as a guide to the background to the use of this term and its relevance to the Nene Valley Railway.

'Load' or 'Loading' Gauge.

There has to be a limiting *profile* - maximum height, width and precise *shape*, in relation to rail height and track centre line - for locomotives, carriages, wagons and other rail vehicles that are to operate over a particular railway line. This is to ensure there is adequate running clearance through tunnels, under bridges, through station platforms, past lineside fixtures and when passing other trains on adjacent tracks. Arched bridges and tunnels present the greatest challenge as their maximum height occurs only at the centre. The traditional British raised station platform (less common on the European Continent, where passengers often have to climb the steps from a low platform or even ground level, to enter carriages) presents another problem. British platforms are usually designed to over-hang towards the track, thus restricting the maximum permissible rail vehicle width from the rail up to platform height. Add to this the effect of a *curved* track and platform in reducing platform edge clearances at the centre, and/or at the leading and trailing corners of each rail vehicle and the effect of vehicles moving at speed and the complexity of the situation becomes apparent.

'Kinetic Structure Gauge'

Relates to the closest allowable proximity to a rail track of bridge and tunnel structures, platform edges, adjacent tracks and general line side 'hardware', to provide the minimum specified clearance for *moving* rail traffic. Thus once a rail line has been built and its 'fixtures' in place, the kinetic structure gauge is set and the appropriate 'load gauge' for that line must then be strictly applied to rail vehicles permitted to run on that route.

UK Load Gauges.

Historically, within the UK, each separate railway company could set its own standards relating to its load gauge. The most restrictive loading gauge is said to have been 12' 8" high x 8' 10" wide. As companies agreed running rights over each others' lines wider standardisation became necessary. Today, British railway engineers and train operators are faced with at least *eight* different load gauges, *applicable to different UK rail routes*, a legacy of the evolution of Britain's railway network coupled with today's need to cater for higher *flat topped* containers and 'piggy-back' rail freight traffic at home and to and from the European Continent. These load gauges, in ascending order of 'size' are designated 'Smaller than W6', W6, W7, W8, W9, W10, W12 and W18.

European Load Gauges.
On the European Continent, where from early days trains would run through several countries, the original 'European' agreed load gauge of 1891 was based upon the French standard, the smallest with respect to height and width. Most other European countries had higher load gauges than the French so this first attempt at standardising was a restricting compromise from the outset. Whilst the 'lower' French trains could pass through almost any country, other countries' trains were severely restricted in travelling through France.

In 1913 a major attempt was made to arrive at a 'better' internationally-agreed load gauge. A conference was held in Berne, Switzerland, the outcome of which was a new load gauge, 14' 0 $^1/_2$" x 10' 4" wide, a mere 2" wider and just less than 5 $^1/_4$" higher than the original 1891 European standard.

Sometimes referred to as the Universal Gauge this new standard was officially designated the Gabrit Passe-Partout Internationale, or PPI, which literally translates into 'pass everywhere international gauge'. The agreement was signed at the end of the Conference and came into force on 1st January 1914.

The new gauge became known *unofficially* in the UK as the Berne Convention Gauge, or simply the 'Berne' Gauge.

Far from solving the international load gauge problem the 'Berne' Gauge merely frustrated it, for other European countries had existing load gauges that were considerably higher and/or wider. These continued in use in the regions involved under the auspices of the Union of Central European Railway Administrations. The Scandinavian load gauge had always been wider than that of other European countries, so standard Swedish and Norwegian coaches could not in general run throughout the rest of Europe.

With the eventual creation of the International Union of Railways (UIC - Union International des Chemins de Fer), of which Britain's four main line railways were members, steps were taken to rationalise the international multitude of load gauges. The UIC 'A' gauge was formulated, slightly higher than the original 'PPI' (Berne) gauge. UIC 'B' and 'C' gauges are higher still, to accommodate the existing gauges in other countries.

Although the UK is a member of UIC, British load gauges W6 to W9 are considerably smaller than UIC standards, all being lower at rail centre-line and with traditional curved top profiles to 'tuck' under bridge and tunnel arches. W10 to W18 are progressively higher at rail centre-line and are more flat-topped. The diagram on page 120 shows only the UK W6 load gauge, in comparison with the four continental gauges. It will be seen that UIC 'A' and 'B' gauges are only marginally higher than the original 1914 Universal gauge but have flatter top profiles.

Only UIC 'C' is considerably higher than the others and almost fully flat-topped. The European route availability of UIC 'C' is strictly limited.

There is little difference in width between the UIC gauges, but it should be noted that UIC vehicle width extends down almost to rail level. As mentioned earlier, however, the traditional British high, over hanging station platform, poses a width restriction from rail level up to platform height (see diagram on page 120).

Because of the way in which UIC vehicle widths are defined in relation to length (to allow for the effect of 'end throw' and 'centre throw' on curved track) the standard 26m - long UIC passenger coach now has to be no more than 2,825 mm (9' 3") wide - which, incidentally, is the width over door handles of a BR Mk. 1 coach. This is a simplification of the International Load Gauge scenario.

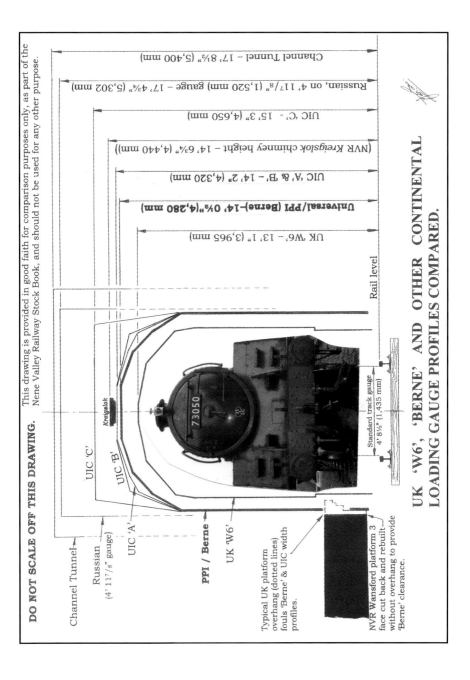

DO NOT SCALE OFF THIS DRAWING. This drawing is provided in good faith for comparison purposes only, as part of the Nene Valley Railway Stock Book, and should not be used for any other purpose.

Channel Tunnel – 17' 8½" (5,400 mm)

Russian, on 4' 11⁷/₈" (1,520 mm) gauge – 17' 4¾" (5,302 mm)

UIC 'C' – 15' 3" (4,650 mm)

(NVR *Kriegslok* chimney height – 14' 6¾" (4,440 mm))

UIC 'A' & 'B' – 14' 2" (4,320 mm)

Universal/PPI (Berne)–14' 0¾"(4,280 mm)

UK 'W6' – 13' 1" (3,965 mm)

Rail level

Channel Tunnel

Russian
(4' 11⁷/₈" gauge)

UIC 'C'

UIC 'B'

UIC 'A'

PPI / Berne

UK 'W6'

Kriegslok

73050

Standard track gauge
4' 8½" (1,435 mm)

Typical UK platform
overhang (dotted lines)
fouls 'Berne' & UIC width
profiles.

NVR Wansford platform 3
face cut back and rebuilt
without overhang to provide
'Berne' clearance.

UK 'W6', 'BERNE' AND OTHER CONTINENTAL
LOADING GAUGE PROFILES COMPARED.

119

How the Nene Valley Railway has adapted to the 'Berne' Gauge.

Although the original Northampton - Peterborough Railway was initially laid down (1843-45) as a single-track line, all structures were built for double track and the railway was doubled shortly after opening. This fact alone has enabled the present Nene Valley Railway, *as a single track line,* to adapt more easily to meet the requirements of higher and wider Continental locomotives and rolling stock, in accordance with the requirements of HSE Railway Inspectorate.

It may be stating the obvious but a close watch has to be kept on all rail levels and on track re-laying work under bridges and through tunnels, as too much ballast will raise the rail level excessively and reduce overhead clearance, arched bridges and tunnels being the most vulnerable.

Travelling eastwards from Yarwell Junction (where the new platform to be built in Autumn 2006 will be fully Berne-compliant) towards Peterborough on the present Nene Valley Railway -

Wansford Tunnel.

The original twin-track single bore, built to generous dimensions to compensate for the lack of ventilation shafts, provides just enough clearance even with both tracks still in place, to accommodate Continental rolling stock running *on the single running line,* but with only British rolling stock *standing* on the adjacent line, (now a siding). A *'Limit of Berne'* sign on the siding at the tunnel eastern entrance clearly sets out this prohibition. HMRI agreed the dynamic clearances on the running line subject to a 15 mph permanent speed restriction and subject to Continental coaches having restricted movement on their opening windows due to the reduced clearance to tunnel wall at cant rail level.

Great North Road (A1) Over Bridge.

This dual carriageway over bridge was built circa 1956. Its flat soffit presents neither height nor lateral clearance problems for Continental stock.

Wansford Station Platforms 2 and 3.

The original 'old station' platform, now NVR platform 3, with its traditional overhang, was too close to the existing ex-BR running line to accept Continental rolling stock. To correct this, in conformity with Berne standards, the platform wall (i.e. from track bed level upwards) was cut back by a nominal 223 mm (approx. 9") and the platform face rebuilt, i.e. the platform was narrowed by this amount. Under agreement with HMRI the existing platform height was retained, for use with both British and Continental coaching stock. The running line was left in situ, the track geometry unaffected.

This platform reconfiguration, to accommodate both British and Continental coaching stock, resulted in a slightly wider gap for passengers to cross when entering the British coaches. NVR's DMU needed to be fitted with wider steps to ensure correct 'stepping distance' compliance. Furthermore, to allow for the 'inset' steps on certain of the Continental vehicles, NVR provides 'loading boards' for passengers' use when required.

On double tracks, the track centre-line distance needs to be increased from the British standard centres to a minimum of 3,600 mm (approx. 11' 9³/₄") to accept 'Berne' rolling stock *running* on both tracks. Consequently, prior to building the new platform 2, its track, already in place, was slewed over by approx. 8" to achieve this dimension in relation to the track serving platform 3.

Castor Mill Lane Over Bridge (No. 62).
Here, adequate height is provided by the existing arched profile of the bridge, without the need to slew the track.

Lynch River Under Bridge (No. 63).
The box-section side girders on this bridge rise well above rail level resulting in reduced clearance at the sides of the wider Continental coaches. To allow for this intrusion into the 'kinetic envelope' for the structure gauge, as well as to preserve the integrity of the bridge structure, a permanent speed restriction of 10 mph is imposed on *all* trains passing over this bridge, although it is only the Continental rolling stock that is subject to reduced clearance.

Lynch Farm Over Bridge (Earl Fitzwilliam's Bridge).
This was a 'flat' cast iron bridge, one of the most ornate bridges on the line. However, its very limited height above rail level lead to the decision in 1974, to remove the bridge span altogether to permit the use of Continental stock. The remains of the bridge piers can still be seen.

Lynch Farm Over Bridge (No. 65).
The original bridge structure provided adequate Berne clearance for the opening of the NVR in 1977. However, a later request to bring an ex-DR 2-10-0 *Kriegslok* locomotive (see page 24), built in excess of the Berne gauge, to the Railway, resulted in a track slew of 500 mm (approx. $19^3/_4$") to provide adequate clearance to the underside of the double track arch.

Travelling eastwards beyond this point all NVR structures, including the platforms at Ferry Meadows, Orton Mere and Peterborough Nene Valley stations and the dual carriageway over bridge at Orton Mere were newly built with adequate clearances provided for Continental rolling stock.

As a matter of further interest* -
The USA has the largest loading gauge, for standard-gauge track, in the world at 15' 6" high and 10' 9" wide.

The world's largest loading gauge (excepting the Channel Tunnel) is on the Russian 4' $11^7/_8$" gauge track - 17' $4^3/_4$" high and 11' 2" wide.

The Australian standard gauge lines' loading gauge is 14' 0" and 10' 6" approx. the same as the 1913 PPI (Berne) gauge.

The Channel Tunnel has the world's largest-of-all loading gauges at 17' $8^1/_2$" high and 13' $1^1/_2$" wide.

* Source for this section only: The Guinness Book of Railway Feats and Facts.

Locomotives and Vehicles that have left the Nene Valley Railway

Steam Locomotives	Period on NVR	2006 Location
No. 70000. 'Britannia'. BR Class 7MT 4-6-2	1980-2000	Crewe
No. 80-014. DB Class 80 0-6-0T	1981-1997	Holland
No. 740. DSB Class S 2-6-4T	1980-1995	Denmark
No. 5231. LMS 'Black Five' 4-6-0	1988-1993	Ropley
No. 2248 -90432. Barclay 0-4-0ST	1972-1991	Sheperdswell
No. 1928 'Alan Gladden' SJ Class S1 2-6-4T	1973-1989	Tonbridge Wells
No. 2000. Peckett 0-6-0ST	1977-1984	Barrow Hill
No. 1917 'Pitsford' .Avonside 0-6-0ST	1973-1983	Elsecar Steam Railway
No. 3837 'Corby No.16' Hawthorn Leslie 0-6-0ST	1974-1981	Leatherhead
No. 1604. Hudswell Clarke 0-6-0ST	1975-1981	Wetheringsett
No. 1908 'Fred' Avonside 0-4-0ST	1976-1981	Dendermonde, Belgium
No. 1844. Hudswell Clarke 0-6-0T	1976-1980	Scrapped (spares)
No. 841 'Greene King' SR Class S15 4-6-0	1977-1978	Grosmont
No. 34081 '92 Squadron' Battle of Britain 4-6-2	1975-2004	North Norfolk Rly

Diesel Locomotives.		
No. 2894. 'Percy' Hibbert 0-4-0	1972-2006	Norfolk
No.31108. BR Class 31 A1A-A1A	2001-2005	Butterley
D9529 '14029'. BR Class 14 0-6-0DH	1988-2000	Beechbrook Farm
D2112. BR Class 03 0-6-0DM	1991-1998	Boston Docks
No. 08704. BR Class 08 0-6-0 DE	1993-1997	Boston Docks
No. 319294. Ruston & Hornsby DS165 0-6-0DM	1991-1996	Hunsbury Hill
No. 4220033 John Fowler 0-4-0DH	1991-1996	Hunsbury Hill
D7594. BR Class 25 Bo-Bo DE	1992-1994	K & ES Railway
No. 804. Alco	1986-1991	Railworld
No. 8368 'Horsa' RSH 262 hp 0-4-0DH	1980-1991	East Dereham
No. 294268 Ruston & Hornsby DS48 4wDM	1975-1991	Sheperdswell
No. 321734 Ruston & Hornsby DS88 4wDM	1979-1991	Sheperdswell
D2089 BR Class 03 0-6-0DM	1991	Burnham-on-Crouch
No. 1212. SJ Class Y7 Diesel Railcar	1984-1989	Fleggburgh
D9016 'Gordon Highlander' BR Class 55 Co-Co DE	1984-1989	Tyseley
D9000 'Royal Scots Grey' BR Class 55 Co-Co DE	1983-1986	Barrow Hill
D615 Hudswell Clarke 153 hp 0-6-0DM	1977-1978	Toddington

Rolling Stock.		
50 8629-26 482-3 (NVR 474) DSB CLL	1983-2006	Wittering
DB992164 BR Trout	19??-2006	Rutland (on loan)
691535 LMS 20T Hopper	19??-2006	Rutland (on loan)
87537 BR Insul-Fish	1977-2005	Location unknown
4615 BR Mk. 1 TSO	1983-2005	North Norfolk Ry.
4667 BR Mk.1 TSO	1983-2005	North Norfolk Ry.

Rolling Stock	Period on NVR	2006 Location
DE320882 Crane Runner for 274	1981-2004	Chasewater
274 BR 10 ton Crane	1981-2004	Chasewater
E168064 LNER 20 ton Brake	? -2004	Chasewater
M730302 LMS 20 ton Brake	? -2004	Chasewater
B891988 BR Cattle Wagon	? -2004	Chasewater
1727 GNR 6-wheeled Express Brake Van	? -2003	Quainton Road
B702702 BR 11 ton Conflat Wagon	1991-2000	Location unknown
13228 BR Mk. 1 FK1693 BR Mk. 1 RB	? -1999	Butterley
1693 BR Mk. 1 RB (Used in London's Burning)	1997-1999	Ruddington (scrapped)
W316W BR(W) Hawksworth BG	1978-1998	Didcot
RW483 LT Bogie Flat Rail Wagon	1994-1997	Location unknown
14623 GWR $3^1/_2$ ton Crane	1974-1996	Huddersfield
S50 Blackburn Meadows Sewage Works Sheffield Side Tipping Wagon	1993-1994	Cottesmore
11187 SR MBSO Unit 3135 4-COR	1981-1993	St. Leonards
B530606 BR 14 ton Conflat Wagon	1991-1992	Wheeting
977091 BR/Leyland Experimental Vehicle	1986-1991	Shepherdswell (loan)
P82261 BSC 7-plank Open Wagon	1982-1991	Shepherdswell
290 Pullman MBSO Unit 3052 5-BEL	1979-1990	E. Lancs Ry. (Scrapped)
46140 BR Mk. 1 Second	1990	Scrapped
Thomas Smith & Sons 5 ton Diesel Crane	1979-199?	Scrapped
337 BR Pullman PKSO	1981-1987	Carnforth
37011 LMS CCT. Lot No. 1091	1977-1986	K & ES Railway
11825 SR TCK Unit 3135 4-COR	1976-1986	Sheffield Park
11201 SR MBSO Unit 3142 4-COR	1976-1986	Horsted Keynes
10096 SR TSK Unit 3142 4-COR	1976-1986	Sheffield Park
11161 SR MBSO Unit 3142 4-COR	1976-1986	Sheffield Park
11773 SR TCK Unit 3017 6-PUL	1976-1984	Swanage (Scrapped)
1798 GNR BTK	1976-1983	Kirkby Stephen
6118 LNER RTO	1976-1983	Carnforth
42972 LNER TOP	1976-1983	Burnham-on-Crouch
21772 LNER TO	1976-1983	Carnforth (Scrapped)
32991 LMS BG (Body cut up 1983-84/frames to K &ESR.	1977-1978	(Frames re-used, body scrapped)
11756 Thomas Smith & Sons 5 ton Steam Crane	1973-1982	Scrapped
48001 BR Mk. 1 SLO	1979-1982	Churnet Valley Ry.
43043 BR Mk. 1 CL	1979-1982	Loughborough
278 'Bertha' Pullman Kitchen Car	1976-1980	Carnforth
1805 LMS TO	1978-1979	Location unknown
46141 BR Mk. 1 S (used in TV crash scene)	1976-1979 &1 990	Padiham (scrapped '94)
15296 BR Mk. 1 CK	1974-1979	Loughborough. Scr.1987
15514 BR Mk. 1 CK	1975-1979	Loughborough. Scr.1987
24656 BR Mk. 1 SK	1977-1979	Loughborough. Scr.1994
4914 BR Mk. 1 TSO	1977-1979	Loughborough.
43140 BR Mk. 1 BS	1976-1979	Shepherdswell
62565 LNER BTK	1975-1976	Loughborough

Visiting Locomotives - Steam

This is a list of steam locomotives that have worked on NVR metals over a period of years, hired to create extra attractions and to give visitors a sight of something unusual and recently providing servicing for Network Rail passed Locomotives. Usual base might not be up to date but correct when locomotive visited the NVR. Further information added when acquired. (This list is not exhaustive - any further information would be welcomed).

Period	Description/Number/Name	Usual Base
Summer 1988	GWR Class 61XX No. 6106. 0-6-2T.	Didcot
1989 Season	GWR Class 28XX No. 3822. 2-8-0.	Didcot
Sept 1990-June 1991	Avonside Engine Co. No. 1973. 'Dora'. 0-4-ST	Cottesmore
Winter 91/92	Andrew Barclay No. 2139. 'Salmon'. 0-6-0ST.	Cottesmore
Sept. 1992	Aveling & Porter No. 8800. 'Sir Vincent'. 4wWT.	Hunsbury Hill
March 1993	'Locomotion' (replica). 0-4-0.	Beamish
1993 Season	LNER Class N7 No. 69621.	Chappel & Wakes Colne.
Early Summer 1993	Aveling & Porter No. 8800. 'Sir Vincent'. 4wWT.	Hunsbury Hill
Late Summer 1993	GWR Class 94XX No. 9466. 0-6-0PT.	Quainton Road
1994 Season	GWR Manor Class No. 7819 'Hinton Manor'. 4-6-0.	Bridgnorth
Early Summer 1994	LNER Class A3 No. 60103 'Flying Scotsman'. 4-6-2.	Southall
August 1994	Avonside Engine Co. No. 1973. 'Dora'. 0-4-ST	Cottesmore
Late Summer 1994	Aveling & Porter No. 8800. 'Sir Vincent'. 4wWT.	Hunsbury Hill
Oct 29 & 30 1994 (Railtour)	LNER Class A4 No. 60009 'Union of South Africa'. 4-6-2.	Makrinch
1995 Season	LNER K4 Class No. 3442 'Great Marquess'. 2-6-0.	Bridgnorth
June 1995	'Locomotion' (replica). 0-4-0.	Beamish
June 1995	SR Merchant Navy Class No. 35005 'Canadian Pacific'. 4-6-2.	Loughborough
June 1995	LNER Class Y1 No. 68153. 4wVBT.	Middleton
June 1995	Aveling & Porter No. 8800. 'Sir Vincent'. 4wWT.	Hunsbury Hill
June 1995	Aveling & Porter No. 9449 'Blue Circle'. 2-2-0T.	Hunsbury Hill
Late Summer 1995	LMS Jubilee Class No. 45596 'Bahamas'. 4-6-0.	Ingrow
Late Summer 1995	LNER Class A4 No. 60007 'Sir Nigel Gresley'. 4-6-2.	Grosmont
Winter 1995/1996	LMS Class 5 No. 44767 'George Stephenson'. 4-6-0.	Grosmont
June & Sept.1996	Cockerill No. 2945 'Yvonne'. 0-4-0VBT.	Hunsbury Hill
Winter 1996	LNER Class A4 No. 60009 'Union of South Africa'.	Makrinch
21 Apl 97 (Railtour)	LNER Class A2 No. 60532 'Blue Peter'. 4-6-2.	Grosmont
Summer 1997	LMS Class 8P No.46229 'Duchess of Hamilton'4-6-2.	York
Summer 1997	Cockerill No. 2945 'Yvonne'. 0-4-0VBT.	Hunsbury Hill
Summer 1997	Aveling & Porter No. 8800. 'Sir Vincent'. 4wWT.	Hunsbury Hill
Summer 1997	LMS Class 5MT 45337	Bury
August 1997	Sentinel No. 9537. 'Susan.' 4wVBT.	Quainton Road
Spring 1998	LNER Class J27 No. 65894 0-6-0	Grosmont
July 1998	SR West Country Class No. 34027 'Taw Valley'.4-6-2.	Grosmont
Summer 1998	LNER/GNR Class J52 No. 68846. 0-6-2ST.	Barrow Hill
Winter 1998/99	GWR Hall Class No. 4920 'Dumbleton Hall'. 4-6-0.	Buckfastleigh
September 1999	LNER Class V2 No. 60800 'Green Arrow'. 2-6-2.	York
Feb '02/03/04/05	Avonside Engine Co. No. 1973. 'Dora'. 0-4-ST.	Cottesmore
Summer 2002	GWR Class 43XX No. 5224. 2-8-0T.	Loughborough
5 Apl 03 (Railtour)	BR Class 5 No. 73096. 4-6-0.	Ropley
Winter 2004/05	LMS Class 5MT 45337	Bury
Spring 2005-06	Cockerill No. 2945 'Yvonne'. 0-4-0VBT.	Hunsbury Hill

Visiting Locomotives - Steam - Continued

Period	Description/Number/Name	Usual Base
Summer 2005	GWR Class 94XX No. 9466. 0-6-0PT.	Quainton Road
18/19 Oct 2005	LNER Class A4 No. 60009 'Union of South Africa'.	Makrinch
3 - 5 Oct 2005	LMS Class 5 No. 45231. 4-6-0.	Ropley
31 Mch - 1 Apl 2006	LNER Class B1 No. 61264. 4-6-0.	Barrow Hill

Visiting Locomotives - Diesel

This list shows diesel motive power that has worked onto NVR metals.

Between "Eurosteam 80" and "Eurosteam 86" a DMU shuttle was in service between Peterborough North and Orton Mere via the Fletton loop, many first generation DMU's being used to operate the service. Where there is an entry under 'Usual Base' this is at the time of the visit - it would be impossible to keep a track of the present locations due to constant movement of stock.

This list is not exhaustive and any further information would be welcomed at the Wansford office.

Symbols used in this list:- $ indicates item scrapped. # indicates renumbered later.

Period	Number/Name	Usual Base
11 April 1978	**31 169**	BR $
27 Dec 1980	**46 044** (Railtour)	BR $
4 May 1981	**55 002 "The King's Own Yorkshire Light Infantry"** (Railtour).	BR (Preserved York).
25 May 1981	**55 009 Deltic. "Alycidon"** (Railtour).	BR Preserved Barrow Hill.
25/26 June1981	**31 411**	BR #$
25/26 June 1981	**37 121**	BR #
12 Sept 1981	**55 007 "Pinza"** (Railtour).	BR $
19 Sept 1981	**08 438** (on shuttle service).	BR
1 May 1982	**40 081** (Railtour).	BR $
1 May 1982	**40 012 Aureol"** (Railtour with 40 081).	BR (Preserved at Butterley).
3 May 1982	**40 013 "Adania"** (Railtour).	BR (Preserved Barrow Hill).
31 July 1982	**31 118**	BR $
11 Dec 1982	**47 431** (Railtour).	BR $
3 Dec 1983	**47 527** (Railtour).	BR $
12 May 1985	**47 016** (Railtour).	BR $
27 May 1985	**47 424** (Hauling The Orient Express).	BR $
26 April 1986	**53907, 59592, 53854, 53818, 59115, 53193.** (Railtour).	BR 2 x 3 car DMU.
29 April 1986.	**DR 73-435.**	BR Track Tamper.
20 Sept 1986.	**150 109** (On shuttle service).	BR Sprinter Class 150/1 DMU.
11 April 1987.	**33 008 "Eastleigh"** (Hauling the Orient Express).	BR (Preserved Shacklestone).
28 Nov 1987	**51679, 54257, 51866, 54274, 54491, 51855, 51654, 54222** (Railtour).	BR 4 x 2 car DMU

Visiting Locomotives - Diesel - Continued

Period	Number/Name	Usual Base
9 Oct 1988	**54081, 51937** (Railtour).	BR 2 car DMU.
24 April 1989	**47 653** (Officer's Special).	BR#
Sept '89/Sept '90	**D2112 Class 03 0-6-0DM** (Gala).	BSC Peterborough.
Oct 1990	**45 133** (Gala).	Butterley.
Oct 1990	**55 015 (Deltic) "Tulyar"** (Gala).	Butterley.
Oct 1990	**D1013 "Western Ranger" Class 52 "WESTERN" C-C DH** (Gala).	Bridgenorth.
March 1991	**DR 73-435/DR 73-431**	BR Track Tampers.
21 Oct 1991	**47 217** (Hauled 7MT "Britannia").	BR $
9 July 1992	**31 417** (Collected D306) Doncaster Open Day.	BR $
19 April 1993	**31 553** (Hauled 7MT "Britannia" & "Queen of Scots" Coaches).	BR $
22 April 1993	**20 902 "Lorna"** (Weedkilling train).	Kilmarnock.
22 April 1993	**20 903 "Alison"** (Weedkilling train).	Kilmarnock.
10 May 1993	**31 552** (Collected stock for Ruislip Open Day).	BR #
18 May 1993	**47 671** (Returning stock from Ruislip Open Day).	BR
6 July 1993	**31 541** (Contract work at Yacht Club Crossing).	BR $
9 Sept 1993	**33 116** (Collected "Queen of Scots" Coaches).	BR (Preserved Loughborough).
1 - 2 Oct 1993	**37 379** (Diesel Gala).	BR
11 Jan 1994	**DR 77-323**	BR Track Tamper.
14 Jan 1994	**47 331** plus continuous welded rail unit **DR 89-009**. (BR training - In).	BR
27 Jan 1994	**47 676 "Northamptonshire"** (Collecting DR 89-009)	BR
19 Feb 1994	**51345, 51387, 51401, 51359** (Railtour)	BR 2 x 2 car DMU (51401 now on NVR).
21 - 23 March 1994.	**31 558 "Nene Valley Railway"** (naming special and loco repaint).	BR $
27 July 1994	**31 541 & 41 5196 (Class 415 x 4 car EMU Type EPB)** (For filming).	BR $
26 July 1994	**31 461** (Collecting 41 5196)	BR
8 - 9 Oct 1994.	**58 049 "Littleton Colliery"** (Gala).	BR
14 Jan 1995	**47 820** (Railtour).	BR #
Spring 1995.	**20 188** as Russian 715-5623 (James Bond 'GoldenEye' filming).	Crewe.
June 1995	**58 023 "Peterborough Depot"** (Gala).	Mainline Freight.
June 1995	**31 558 "Nene Valley Railway"** (Gala).	Mainline Freight.
15 - 17 Sept 1995.	**31 165** (Gala).	Mainline Freight $
9 May 1996.	**20 902 "Lorna" and 20 903 "Alison"** (Weedkilling Train).	Kilmarnock.
25 Sept 1996.	**31 271** (Ballast Train).	Mainline Freight (Preserved).
Autumn '96	**DR73-426, 73-427 and 77-330.**	Scottish TRU Track Machines.
7 Dec 1996.	**37 293** (Collects A4 No. 60009 support coach 99405).	Mainline Freight.

Period	Number/Name	Usual Base
14 Feb 1997	37 427 (Delivering coaches for filming "London's Burning").	EWS
3 March 1997	37 427 (Collecting coaches from filming "London's Burning").	EWS
8 Sept 1998	31 466 (Ballast train).	EWS
1999 Season.	**5580 (31 162) Class 31 A1A-A1A DE.**	A1A Loco Group Butterley.
24 July 2000	47 744 (Collecting Class 31 No. 5580)	EWS
9 Sept 2000	67 004 "Post Haste" (Naming).	EWS
18 - 19 Oct 2000	31 110 "Traction" (Ballast train)	EWS $
Nov/Dec 2000	DR80 - 210 and 80 - 212 (Track Machine testing),	Railtrack.
21 April 2001	60 015 and 56 055 (Railtour).	EWS
2001 Season.	**55 019 Deltic "Royal Highland Fusilier"**	DPS Barrow Hill
17-18 Sept 2001	**D172 Class 46 'Peak' "Ixion" 1 Co-Co1 DE**	Crewe
17-18 Sept 2001	**5580 Class 31 A1A-A1A DE** (Delivering 31 108)	A1A Loco Group Butterley.
5 Jan 2002	**D9000 "Royal Scots Grey" Class 55 Deltic Co-Co DE.** (Railtour)	D9000 Loco Gp. Stewarts Lane
May &June 2002	**47 401**	Butterley.
	55 019, D9009 "Alycidon" Class 55 "Deltic" Co-Co DE.	Barrow Hill.
8/9 July 2002	**47 150**	Freightliner,
	66 705 "Golden Jubilee" (Railtrack filming).	GBRf.
26 April 2003	**66 706 "Nene Valley"** (Naming).	GBRf. Rotherham
24 Sept 2003	**66 706 "Nene Valley"**	(Industrial).
21 Nov 03 - /Dec 03	**No. 491 Andrew Barclay 0-6-0DH** (Maintenance).	GBRf.
9/10 Oct 2004.	**66 709 "Joseph Arnold Davies"** (Gala).	GBRf
11 May 2005	**66 702 "Blue Lightening"** (Delivering 31 271, collecting 31 108).	GBRf
16 - 18 Sept 2005.	**73 206 "Lisa",**	GBRf
18 March 2006.	**73 209 "Alison"**	GBRf
	66 558 (Gala).	Freightliner.
	66 714 "Cromer Lifeboat" (Self Discharge Ballast Train - Yarwell Project).	GBRf.
4 + 5 April 2006	**66 713 "Norwich City"** (Army Driver Training).	GBRf.
4 - 6 June 2006.	**66 711** (Metronet Driver Training).	GBRf.
19 + 20 June 2006.	**66 718** (Metronet Driver Training).	GBRf Metronet.
26 + 27 June 2006.	**66 710** (Metronet Driver Training).	GBRf.
3 + 4 July 2006	**66 706 "Nene Valley"** (Metronet Driver Training).	GBRf.
4 Aug 2006.	**DR73-435**	Fastline Tamper.
12/9/06 - 10/06.	**56 003** (Gala).	Privately Owned
13 Sept 2006.	**66 716 "Willesden Traincare Centre".**	GBRf.
Oct 2006	**27 066** (Gala).	Lydney.

PIPE TRAINS

The Pipe Trains consisted of 27 BDA 58 ton Bogie Steel Wagons weighing approximately 900 tons, carrying 4 pipes per wagon. These trains worked from Leith to Yarwell with EWS bringing the train to Orton Mere. From Orton Mere to Yarwell on NVR metals, they were hauled by a Class 14.

The EWS locomotives used were as follows:-

Date	Loco No/Name
16 March 1998	60 065 "Kinder Law"
17 March 1998	60 080 "Kinder Scout"
18 March 1998	60 047
19 March 1998	60 025
20 March 1998	56 103 "Stora"
20 March 1998	56 031
1 April 1998	60 042
2 April 1998	60 078
3 April 1998	37 198
6 April 1998	60 025
7 April 1998	60 078
8 April 1998	60 027
9 April 1998	60 078
9 April 1998	56 108
22 April 1998	60 050
23 April 1998	60 052
24 April 1998	60 010
24 April 1998	37 025 "Inverness TMD"
28 April 1998	60 076
29 April 1998	60 005
30 April 1998	60 018
1 May 1998	56 050 "British Steel Teeside"

Class 60 No. 60 050 with a Class 14 hauling the pipe train in the background on 22nd April 2006. Photo: David Harrison.